RESCUE PILOT

CHEATING THE SEA

JERRY GRAYSON, AFC

ADLARD COLES NAUTICAL

B L O O M S B U R Y

LONDON • NEW DELHI • NEW YORK • SYDNEY

Dedicated to the memory of John Carpenter, a superb helicopter engineer who taught us all the true meaning of bravery.

Adlard Coles Nautical
An imprint of Bloomsbury Publishing Plc

50 Bedford Square	1385 Broadway
London	New York
WC1B 3DP	NY 10018
UK	USA

www.bloomsbury.com

ADLARD COLES, ADLARD COLES ~~~~~~ ırks
of Blooms
First publi
First publis

© Jerry Gra

Jerry Grays   , 1988,
to be identi

All rights re   1 any
form or by ɛ   ɜ, or
any informa   ›m the
publishers.

No responsil   ining
from action   bury
or the author

British Library Cataloguing-in-Publication Data
A catalogue record for this book is available from the British Library.

Library of Congress Cataloguing-in-Publication data has been applied for.

ISBNs
978-1-4729-1794-2 (paperback)
978-1-4729-1795-9 (ePub)
978-1-4729-1796-6 (ePDF)

10 9 8 7 6 5 4 3 2 1

Typeset in Haarlemmer MT by MPS Limited
Printed and bound in Great Britain by CPI Group (UK) Ltd, Croydon CR0 4YY

MIX
Paper from
responsible sources
FSC® C020471

To find out more about our authors and books visit www.bloomsbury.com. Here you will find extracts, author interviews, details of forthcoming events and the option to sign up for our newsletters.

RESCUE
PILOT

CONTENTS

This book by Jerry Grayson, who became the youngest Search and Rescue pilot at the age of just 17 and went on to have a remarkable aviation career within both the Royal Navy and also in the film industry, acts as a reminder of the bravery and selflessness of the crews who put their lives at risk to save others.

Leadership, teamwork and training are the key to success in many fields of endeavour and Search and Rescue flying is just such an endeavour that requires these skills and I know from my own service the importance of all three in creating an effective helicopter crew.

Reading this book I am also reminded of the undeniably strong camaraderie of aviators as well as the wonderful sense of humour that arises in the face of adversity. In recording and celebrating this invaluable work of Search and Rescue, I am certain that this book will be an inspiration for the next generation of pilots.

PROLOGUE

I WAS BORN IN A FOREST near the ancient southern English castle town of Arundel. My mother hadn't known she was pregnant until the day my father delivered me on the table of their modest home, our caravan *Toad Hall*. School was no fun at all; there were so many more interesting things happening just beyond the gates of what I perceived to be a prison. My mum cried when JFK was shot. My dad drove in the Monte Carlo rally. The Rolling Stones were arrested in the next village for some misdemeanour; I didn't understand what the story was about, and I certainly didn't appreciate that we were living through a period of sex, drugs and rock and roll that would change the world forever. All I knew was that everybody else was having a lot of fun while I struggled at school with trigonometry and hormones.

By the time I was twelve I knew I wanted to fly. By the time I was fifteen my maths teacher had regretted admitting that he had a passing interest in aviation: 'Grayson's application to the syllabus can be variable; his discourses on three-dimensional air-traffic systems are a bit much for me at eight o'clock in the morning.' I must have been the worst kind of nerd as I sat for many freezing hours at the end of Gatwick runway glued to the speaker of a little transistor radio, listening to the airliners being seamlessly sequenced to the ground.

By sixteen I had applied to the Royal Navy to fly helicopters. Walking through the doors of Dartmouth Naval College in 1972 might have been a culture shock for the other fifteen officer cadets, most of whom had already lived a bit of life. For me it was just a natural continuation of the schooling process, except that it was designed to end in a cockpit and was therefore worth taking seriously. By seventeen I was able to quote the old self-deprecating military joke: 'Just last month I couldn't spell pilot and now I are one.'

For eight happy years, until 1980, I wore a naval uniform as part of the Fleet Air Arm. I learned how to use a helicopter to chase submarines, and then how to use one to save lives. I entered Civvy Street still with a helicopter on my back. These are my stories. They don't always stick to a strict timeline, because memory doesn't work like that. I've never been one to sweat the dull stuff first; there are too many exciting moments in life that have to be chased down right away. If aviation has taught me nothing else it has taught me that sometimes those highlight events chase *you* down, and often at times when you're least expecting them.

A GREEK PLAY

GOING TO WORK WAS BOTH A THRILL and an ordeal. It was only about a seven-minute ride from home but there was always a feeling of adventure. I would scan the skies as I drove along for an idea of what the day might bring. By the time I'd reached the airbase perimeter track I could make a pretty good guess at the type of work ahead of us. The ordeal came from having to crawl out of my pit in darkness. We had to be in, dressed and ready to go by dawn, which was no small feat in the middle of summer.

Ten days before Christmas 1979 it was very obvious what type of work would come our way. The drive in took much longer than usual as I skirted fallen trees, bits of shed and various other obstacles, some of which were still airborne. Anybody at sea was going to have a very hard time today.

I should explain that 'work' for me consisted of flying a large helicopter with 'Royal Navy' in big letters down the side. It was painted in dark blue with a wide orange dayglo stripe around the tail and an Ace of Clubs high up the side of the main airframe. This colour scheme and logo denoted the helicopter as being one of thirteen similar aircraft, all part of 771 Squadron, responsible for Search and Rescue (SAR) duties around the coast of Cornwall. Our base was the Royal Naval Air Station Culdrose, the biggest helicopter base in Europe, just outside the small town of Helston, deep in the heart of the West Country.

When wearing formal uniform, which I rarely did, the two gold rings around my sleeve denoted the rank of Lieutenant, Royal Navy, and the proudly worn wings placed me as a pilot. Today I was in jeans and sweatshirt, easy garb to throw on in the dark. I would be changing into flying clothing as soon as I reached the squadron office block.

Culdrose was in an appalling state. The airfield was dominated by about a dozen huge oblong hangars. Each hangar could hold about ten big military helicopters and they still looked quite new and shiny – or they had the day before. Overnight the winds had risen to storm force, torn little openings in the roof of each hangar, then systematically set about ripping them to pieces. The walls were still intact but many of the roofs were being peeled back, sheet by sheet. I couldn't believe the size of the corrugated rolls of metal sheeting steadily marching across the grass, down the runway and off into the woods nearby. Each one must have weighed more than a ton.

Our own two hangars had fared better than the rest of them. Our squadron nestled a little way down a valley and was slightly protected by the other squadron hangars further up the slope, but this did mean that we were being bombarded by bits from all the other hangars as they broke up. I chose to break all regulations and park my car in the hangar.

Putting the duty SAR out on the apron was out of the question. It would have been destroyed in minutes. So we prepared it under the big eerie sodium lights inside while the metal-upon-metal sound of the storm raging outside was amplified in the cavernous building.

We didn't have long to wait before the call came in. A Greek cargo vessel, the *Skopelos Sky*, had radioed for immediate assistance: *In position three miles North of Trevose Head. Listing badly. 15 crew members on board.*

Dick Harvey, our coastguard officer, continued listening to the radio as we tried to work out how we were going to get airborne. The Padstow lifeboat was in the process of launching but I didn't fancy their chances of achieving anything in these winds. The waves were likely to be enormous up on the north Cornish coast, a place where, in previous centuries, regular shipwrecks had provided unexpected bounty for the local communities. I had no idea what was on this particular ship and didn't much care. There were fifteen lives at stake and, assuming we could pick them up, we could only carry about seven at a time.

I decided to start up in the hangar. This would be dangerous and would require a good deal of preparation. The big Wessex rotor blades had a diameter of 56 feet and created their own local storm once they were up to full speed. Anything loose in the hangar had to be tied down or moved away. We set about agreeing a series of hand signals from the guys on the ground to coordinate getting the aircraft out of the door and airborne before we were poleaxed by low flying tin.

There were two good reasons for wanting to start in the hangar. The first was obvious: it would reduce the time we'd have to spend on the ground with metal raining down around us. The second has to do with not chopping your own tail off. A helicopter rotor blade is a very carefully made component; it must be both strong and incredibly flexible. When the rotor is turning at full revs each blade gets a good deal of its strength from the centrifugal force, but at low revs it's a different story. At the front of the helicopter very strong gusts have been known to blow the tip of a blade right down to the ground. Rotor blades don't like tarmac – and the feeling seems to be mutual. However, the damage is nothing compared to a blade that's blown upwards at the front. In that event the blade whips back down as it travels round to the rear of the helicopter and smartly chops the whole tail section off. This sends bits of helicopter travelling off by themselves at very high speed, at which point the safest place to be is in the machine rather than anywhere within about a half-mile radius.

While we vacillated over how far out of the hangar we wanted to be before attempting a take-off, Dick Harvey called on the radio. Two RAF helicopters had arrived on scene and were starting to winch up Greek crewmen. This was all the impetus we needed. About 90 seconds later we had cleared the bomb site that used to be Culdrose and were happily being blown towards North Cornwall.

The 'friendly rivalry' between the Navy and the RAF would be better described as 'restrained antagonism'. It goes back a very long way and it's regularly reinforced. The Navy, the Marines and the Army all get on pretty well together. It's something to do with all living in cramped, cold and often wet, dirty and uncomfortable conditions.

The old jokes – such as how the rest of us have traditions but the RAF has been around for less than a century and therefore has only habits – continue to be told from generation to generation. Not many people are aware that there were naval aviators flying from the decks of ships long before anybody had thought of having an air force. An aeroplane was just seen as being another piece of the ship's weaponry.

The wariness with which the Navy regarded the RAF was particularly bad in the mid-1970s. At government cabinet level the senior Crabs (I'm still not sure why we called RAF officers 'Crabs', but we all did) had convinced our lords and masters that aircraft carriers could be phased out and the RAF could henceforth provide the air cover in any theatre of war. Big funding was therefore going their way and we were shortly to be denied our best assets. It's interesting that this was first put to the test five years later in the Falklands, which were so far away from anything that the RAF could fly from that it rather proved the Navy's point. The Crabs were forced to hang around at the mid-Atlantic staging post in the Ascension Islands while the other three services sailed south to get on with the job. At some point the Crabs decided they could help by bombing Port Stanley airfield, at that time in control of the Argentinians. Thirteen big aircraft fuelled a single Vulcan bomber, and then each other, in a complex leapfrog dance to enable them to fly that far, until the bomber reached the target and delivered one of its bombs into the middle of the runway. If only we'd still had the earlier generation *Ark Royal* with her Phantoms, Buccaneers and Gannets to complement the fantastic job done by the Harrier jump jet boys (some of whom, to be fair, were Crab pilots on exchange to the Navy). Thankfully the lesson was learned – it was obvious to those of us at the coalface all along – and has since been partially rectified with the new *Queen Elizabeth* returning to the original concept of a full-sized aircraft carrier.

It was in this context that we headed north to Trevose Head. The Navy SAR basically covered everything around the Cornish coast and sometimes strayed into Devon. The RAF from Chivenor covered most of North Devon and Somerset, and another RAF base at Brawdy covered the south-west peninsula of Wales. Brawdy had sent their bright yellow Sea King with all its sparkly new gear, while Chivenor had sent their dear old Whirlwind, a venerable lady of the skies even older than our Wessex. The Whirlwind wasn't really up to the task in these conditions and soon went home. Once on scene we bowed to the superior Sea King and settled down to watch the fun. A chopper uses far less fuel when it's sitting on the ground with its rotors turning than it does chugging around the sky so we picked ourselves a nice spot on the clifftop and just sat there… and sat there, and sat there. We couldn't stop our rotors in the 70 mph winds; even if we'd survived the shut-down we'd never have got the blades going again without chopping the tail off. So we sat and watched.

Pretty soon there wasn't much to watch. The Crab Sea King had pulled ten seamen off and the Greek vessel's master had decided that he and four others would stay on board to try to save the ship. The Crabs, therefore, went home for breakfast while we watched the *Skopelos Sky* motor up and down the bay. She was certainly listing and I didn't envy the boys left on board. Every wave was a giant one and with each traverse of the bay it seemed she was coming closer and closer inshore.

Two and a half hours went by, then the Sea King came back from breakfast and relieved us on the clifftop while we went for some fuel at RAF St Mawgan. On our approach to the airfield I emphasised my call sign, 'Rescue Two One,' and reiterated the request I'd made as we set off. I wanted a fuel bowser positioned on the runway, clear of any buildings, with its hose laid out and its engine running ready for my arrival. I then wanted a rotors-running (hot) refuel, followed by a bucket of water to throw down my engines. This last request was to clear the thick build-up of salt on my turbine blades, which I knew was happening because my instruments had been showing a steady increase in the internal temperature of the twin Rolls Royce jet engines.

The controller at St Mawgan politely informed me that RAF regulations clearly stipulated that this was contrary to airfield standing order number blah blah blah. I tried another tack: 'St Mawgan, this is *Rescue* Two One. Request the name of the officer taking personal responsibility for the loss of five lives in the event that you refuse to fulfil my requirements.' Miraculously the bowser was waiting for me as I started my approach to the runway and, of course, the man on the ground with the truck was more than happy to do all he could to speed us on our way.

We arrived back at the Clifftop Camp Site For Resting Helicopters and offered to relieve the Sea King. He had, after all, done a great job in picking up ten survivors and I had yet to earn my supper. We received a very kind offer from the Sea King in return: 'Would you chaps like a coffee before we go?' Not half! It was now early afternoon and we'd been scrambled at 0920.

'Thank you, we'd love one. Would you like my crewman to come and get it?'

'No problem. We'll just prepare it and I'll send one of our chaps over with it.'

Prepare it? I had thought he meant he was going to leave his spare thermos behind, but, no, this new beast apparently had some form of catering facilities on board.

After about five minutes of glancing across at this huge 10-ton yellow machine running on the clifftop beside us we saw its big rear door slide open and an RAF crewman jumped to the ground. A colleague carefully passed something down to him and he began the extraordinary task of struggling through storm-force winds balancing a tray on his arm. We couldn't believe it. The surreal nature of the event was compounded when he arrived at our own cabin door. Not only had he successfully brought us four cups of freshly brewed coffee, but there were also four individually wrapped chocolate Club biscuits.

We thanked the Sea King, who duly departed and we settled down for a long afternoon.

Usually we were a crew of three: pilot, diver and crewman, but on this occasion we'd brought the duty doctor with us as well, Sub Lieutenant Waugh. Together the four of us sat, munched, and watched the *Skopelos Sky* continue her fight in what must surely be a losing battle. I was lucky. Not only did I have some of the best professionals on the job with me, but they were also very good company. My diver was Dave 'Wally' Wallace (of whom much more later) and my crewman was Detlef Wodak – on exchange from the Federal German Navy. They'd both been in the job a lot longer than me.

When two or more sailors are gathered together it is decreed that they shall tell stories to each other. I had tears rolling down my face as one story followed another. Through all this I couldn't even see them as I was high up in the pilot's seat holding on to the controls and the other three were way down beneath me in the main cabin under my seat.

Finally, after about five hours sitting in the vibrating seat, the coffee had worked its way through and I was dying to relieve myself. As a procedure carried out in a helicopter, this is not an easy thing. For a start you're dressed in an all-encompassing dry suit, or 'goon suit' as it's universally known. Tight rubber seals surround the wrists and neck, with little rubber booties that fit inside your flying boots. It's an unpleasant garment at the best of times, but after five hours it begins to feel like torture. You can't leave the controls while the rotors are turning; you have to 'fly' the aircraft on the ground. Thankfully the designers had thought of this, even if they hadn't made it easy.

First you have to extricate the required bodily part from the confines of the goon suit, then you have to join it to the pee tube, which is clipped just beneath the pilot's seat. If you use the pee tube the rule is you have to clean out the collection bag yourself when you get back to base. This was not regarded as a fair task to give to the engineers on return. As a result, the pee tube wasn't often used if it could be avoided, but I had no choice.

I undid the horizontal zip and, with something of a struggle, achieved part one of the procedure. Next I unclipped the pee tube and brought the metal contraption up on to my lap. It resembled the old speaking pipes from ancient war-time movies, with a huge stainless steel lid secured with a catch. Meanwhile I carried on the conversation. If the others suspected what I was up to they would have put the on-board camera to good use and I'd never have heard the last of it.

Finally the preparations were complete and all the pain disappeared as I relaxed into the pee tube. Three seconds later an ear-splitting scream came across the intercom followed by other screams, this time of merriment. Mid-conversation the unsuspecting Hauptbootsman Wodak had experienced a hot wet feeling down the back of his neck, then all over the top of his helmet and visor as he struggled to extricate himself from his seat belt. The other two were, of course, clutching their stomachs too hard in mirth to be of any use to him at all. I later learned that a slightly unfortunate sequence of events had led to an engineer declaring: 'We haven't got a replacement pee bag but it won't matter because the pilots never use it anyway.'

Once we'd all settled down again we started to do a few calculations. It would be growing dark before long and there was no way we would be able to lift the five remaining Greeks off in darkness. I'd be putting Wally at too much of a risk. We nipped off to St Mawgan for another quick suck of fuel, having told the Greek captain that we'd be back shortly to begin picking up him and his crew. He couldn't possibly want to stay overnight; it had become increasingly clear that *Skopelos Sky* would be on the rocks before morning. We flew back to the ship and began a bizarre and fragmented conversation over the radio as we tried to convey the seriousness of the circumstances. The conversation went on for a good half hour and so I landed again on the clifftop. We felt uneasy. Whatever we said to the captain, he kept asking for just a little more time to try to save the ship. The rapidly approaching darkness and the difficulties we were undoubtedly going to have in getting them off would sucker us into a set of circumstances in which we'd either lose one of us or several of them.

We tried increasingly blunt statements, but to no effect. I didn't blame him. I was more worried that something was getting lost in translation and I wasn't getting the message across. In the end I resorted to bluff. We took off from the clifftop and I said my farewells to the captain over the radio. 'We wish you great luck and, if you're still afloat in the morning, we'll come back again.' No response. I asked Wally and Detlef to wave from the back door of our aircraft as I flew past the ship one last time. We kept going towards the mainland and held our collective breath. Sure enough, as we crossed the foaming coastline we heard *crackle, crackle, crackle,* 'Rescue Two One we come off now, we come off now please.' I hauled the aircraft round in a tight turn and put the nose down. It was time to go to work and we would have to move fast.

The winds had abated a little. We'd seen them gust to over 110 miles per hour at various stages during the afternoon but they were now down to about 75 mph. In itself this is not a problem for a helicopter; it's just like flying forwards at that speed and not moving across the ground. The problems come from the turbulence, the waves and particularly the various bits of steel that extend upwards from the deck of any ship. The turbulence wasn't too bad as the wind had come round to north-westerly and therefore wasn't hitting any lumps of land before it hit us. The waves were pretty impressive, though, and were throwing the stricken vessel in all directions. With each plunge into a trough the ship would also roll quite viciously, causing the obstructions to flail about as if trying to swat us down from the sky.

I began an approach, wriggled my bottom around in the seat to get comfortable and settled myself into a position where I would be able to keep my body still for the next half hour. Hovering over a ship in a storm is a peculiar activity. Everything around you is moving; the only bit you've got any control over is yourself, so you sit very still and don't move your head. In this way there's no fluid moving in your ear canals and you can rely on yourself as a primary reference point. Beyond that your eyes take in all the other movements that are going on around you and your brain tries to arrive at some sort of conclusion from the information coming in. The waves are going up and down – no problem, let it happen. The ship is going up and down, and side to side – try to anticipate it and go with it, but don't chase it. The horizon is moving – this is very bad as it means the aircraft is changing its attitude (meaning nose up or down) and will shortly therefore change its position.

Amid all this you are about to lower a man at the end of a thin cable on to the deck of the ship. The deck is the one bit of the ship that you can't see because it's directly beneath you, and this is where the teamwork comes in. During the final stages of the approach the crewman starts talking to you – continuously. He's giving you a steady flow of information about your height (which should be reducing), your speed (which should also be reducing) and your position in relation to the bit of the ship that you want to hover over. Once you've arrived in the hover he must keep up the flow, otherwise people are going to get hurt. The crewman's voice replaces your eyes as the primary information source and you sit very still, turning words into pictures in your head before then translating those pictures into tiny movements by each of your hands and by both of your feet; all of which are on the controls. Try it at home: swing a yo-yo around over a spot on the floor and try to keep up a continuous chatter about where the yo-yo is in relation to the spot. Now keep it up for thirty minutes. Oh, and by the way, remembering where Detlef had come from – try it in another language.

We lowered Wally to the deck, me maintaining a hover and Detlef operating the hydraulic winch while all the time keeping up his chatter: 'Height's good, you're drifting forward, come back three, come back two, come back one, steady, come up two, you're drifting

left, come right two, one, steady. Hold that height, the diver is secure, he's at the door, raising the winch, lowering the winch, come back slightly and come up three feet, diver's going down, move forward three to avoid the crane, the diver has ten feet to go, move forward two and left one, five feet to go, hold your height, hold your hover, the ship is coming up now, holding the winch and the diver is three, two, one feet, he's on the deck.'

Now is the most dangerous bit. If you move at all you've got a big problem. If the cable goes taut you'll pull the diver off his feet and probably smash him against some steelwork. If the cable goes slack it is controlled entirely by sod's law which says that it will wrap itself securely around the ship's steelwork. The only way out of this is to immediately cut the cable with an explosive bolt. Do that and you've probably said goodbye to all the people you were trying to pick up, plus your diver (and he's usually the one who is going to cook the supper, so you really don't want to do that).

So, once on deck, Wally immediately released himself from the cable and Detlef called for me to come up and back as he rapidly raised the winch. We could now relax a little and watch Wally clutch his way forward across the heaving deck towards the door at the base of the bridge. Every second or third step he had to hunker down as another big green wave came boiling at him. Eventually he reached the door and… couldn't get it open. He wrenched it, he kicked it, nothing. I called on the radio for them to let him in – nothing, no response at all. I descended lower alongside the ship to try to attract the attention of the crew on the bridge but we couldn't see anybody. Wally was now starting to suffer as wave after wave came crashing along the deck towards him. The divers are all as fit as athletes but they soon tire in the cold and Wally had a lot of work ahead of him. We decided to pick him back up and try to put him on the bridge wing, a tiny balcony that sticks out either side of the bridge and enables the captain to see back down the side of his vessel.

Back into the hover, lower the winch, up came Wally and down again he went as I tried to give Detlef the best chance I could of getting him on to the right spot. He did it and we backed away once more. Wally set off into the bridge and came back with his arms outstretched: he couldn't find anybody. It was getting darker and, with nobody at the wheel, the ship was starting to come around towards the south – in which direction lay the cliffs. For the next part of the saga I have to rely on how Wally told it. He didn't want to venture too far into the ship for fear of getting lost. After a couple of minutes the first sailor appeared on the bridge carrying two suitcases. He handed them to Wally and, astonishingly, ran off to finish his packing. By this time Wally's endless patience and good humour was being severely stretched, but at least he was prepared. As the next sailor appeared on the bridge Wally graciously accepted the suitcases, tossed them over the side into the sea below, grabbed the sailor by the collar and clipped him to the harness. A few moments later he was on his way up the wire towards us. He might have to make a little trip to Marks and Spencer later, but at least we'd got him.

Over the next thirty minutes we managed to save four out of the five remaining crew members. The subsequent Coastguard report reads:

> With the onset of darkness the rescue of the fifth man was abandoned after three attempts when the RAF Sea King with superior hover, flood and winching lights returned to the scene. The Wessex recovered to Royal Naval Air Station Culdrose after a total of 7 hours and 25 minutes of continuous operation. Approximately half an hour later the Sea King winched the Captain off and returned to base.

What the report fails to mention is that the Sea King's crewman suffered quite badly when the ship rolled that little bit too much and

he slammed against the vessel's side before finally managing to haul off the last man. Not a bad day's work for all of us.

Five years later we were all gathered together again at the Greek Consulate in London's Holland Park to receive medals that had never before been awarded outside of Greece. This was much appreciated, but we had to get special permission to wear a foreign medal. The letter in my scrapbook reads:

> Buckingham Palace
>
> Sir,
>
> I have the honour to inform you that the Queen has been graciously pleased to grant you unrestricted permission to wear the Nautical Medal, 1st Class which has been conferred upon you by the Government of the Hellenic Republic in recognition of your services.
>
> I have the honour to be, Sir,
> Your obedient servant.

It was to be another ten years before we finally met one of the survivors when *This Is Your Life* honoured Wally with a well-deserved episode. There was much hugging and crying and I still have no idea if the uninterrupted flow from the Greek sailor's mother was in thanks for her son's life or whether she wanted us to go back and find his suitcase.

THE MIGHTY ARK

THE STORY I'VE JUST TOLD came about during the happy years I spent from 1977 to 1980 as a rescue pilot. Prior to that I had joined the Navy in 1972, learned to wear a uniform, learned to fly, then been posted to 824 Squadron on HMS *Ark Royal*. It was my first 'front line' squadron. We operated Sea Kings in the anti-submarine role. 'Front line' meant we would theoretically be the first to go to war. Thankfully this was not something that ever happened during my eight years serving in the 'Grey Funnel Line' and I was able to use my flying towards better causes, but in theory we were ready. I served twice on the old *Ark*, a magnificent aircraft carrier of over 800 feet which would pulse with life, steam curling upwards from her entire deck when the massive catapults were being used to hurl tons of F4 Phantom fighter jet into the air. She was the Navy's last proper aircraft carrier, by which I mean she was built before the days of the vertical take-off Harrier and the unsightly 'ski-jump' ramp at the front. It was first on *Ark* and then on *Hermes*, a carrier used entirely for helicopters, that I began to learn the skills that would later result in my becoming a rescue pilot.

The BBC made their groundbreaking documentary *Sailor* during the time I was on board. I still hear the title music of Rod Stewart's 'Sailing' whenever I think of the *Ark* and, just like many others, I had tears streaming down my face during the final episode filmed some years afterwards when the Master-at-Arms (the most senior non-officer) found her in a Scottish breakers' yard in the last of her death throes. I say it was groundbreaking because it was only the second time the BBC had used the fly-on-the-wall technique and the first time they'd ever had such access to a military environment. The documentary is still available from the BBC on DVD and I'd highly recommend it as an entirely accurate portrayal of life on board. In the opening titles I'm the one driving the second Sea King in the long line of machines burning and turning on deck: a tiny, invisible cameo but my first taste of television.

A typical deployment (time at sea) would last for around five months. The *Ark* would leave her base in Plymouth and nose her way slowly out into the South West Approaches to the English Channel, where the squadrons would embark. For a shiny new operational pilot, embarkation is a seminal experience. You fly in tight formation over the giant vessel before peeling away one by one to execute your first ever carrier deck landing. The final part of the manoeuvre is assisted by a ground marshaller who uses table tennis bats to indicate a slight hover adjustment required to the left or right, fore or aft, before finally reducing power in order to arrive firmly 'on the spot'. The moment the wheels touch the metal deck, the marshaller in his bright yellow waistcoat calls for chocks and lashings with a crisp inward movement from each of his bats. At this point a pair of chock-heads in drab brown waistcoats rush in from each side, wedge a pair of triangular wooden chocks under each wheel and clip a ratchet lashing between a tough part of the helicopter and a ring-bolt in the deck. In this way the helicopter is prevented from sliding across the deck and over the side – a good precaution on an acreage of metal that is frequently wet and slippery.

The actual moment of landing always needs to be timed carefully, particularly in a rough sea. First you establish a hover off to the port side of the ship. This means you can concentrate on deceleration without any danger of running into anything ahead. If the approach begins to look unsafe, you resume forward flight and go around again. Once in the hover the helicopter speed is matched to the ship's speed, with the ocean rushing past at around 30 knots. You then hover to the right and over the deck. At that point you are already timing rise and fall to match the pitch of the ship. In a rough sea the deck could be rising or falling by as much as 60 feet and this is accentuated the further towards the stern your allocated spot is. When hovering at 10 to 15 feet, a 60-foot variation is a big deal and it requires great concentration to match your flight path up and down with the ship's motion. It is a case of timing the landing to coincide with the peak of the deck's movement. If you timed it right you could kiss the wheels on to the deck just as she started to go down into the next trough. Time it wrong and a descending helicopter would meet a rapidly rising deck. The undercarriage of any Naval aircraft is considerably more beefy than any land-based equivalent but you could still almost hear the machine exhale painfully if you slammed her on to the deck too hard.

So, with chocks and lashings firmly in place, you could shut down the engines and rotors without fear of losing the aircraft, but the first on deck waited before doing this until the next helicopter had landed in order not to suffer from his downwash just as your own rotors were beginning to slow their rotation and lose their rigidity. During a mass embarkation of the whole squadron this would often result in a line-up of eight Sea Kings simultaneously burning and turning on deck, a sight certain to stir excitement through a young pilot, and at this stage I was still only 19 years old.

As you stepped down on to the deck of the huge and majestic old lady, thoughts of another life elsewhere were banished. This would be home for the next five months. The size of the deck made it impossible to see over more than one edge at a time so you were almost isolated from the fact that you were on a ship. It was more like being on the surface of another planet, and the steam coming from the catapults towards the bow only added to that impression.

Towering over everything was the island, the superstructure that formed the nerve centre of all the ship's operations. The most obvious part of the island was the bridge, the lofty domain of the captain and his hierarchy of seamen officers. This was the place where even the simplest command to alter course was given and received formally and precisely. Just as in the cockpit of an aircraft or helicopter, each person on the bridge knew their role, knew their place and took pride in their job as part of a team. But to an aviator, the bridge represented the mysterious world of the real Navy and as such was an area to be avoided.

The island also contained, a few levels down, the operations room, which was darkened, hushed and illuminated only by the glow from radar screens. At some point during our training I guess we had studied the structure of the roles in the operations room and probably even sat some exams on the subject, but for a pilot it was, once again, a place to be avoided for fear of inadvertently transgressing some rule of formal conduct.

Next to the ops room was the door to the ACRB (Air Crew Refreshment Bar). This was a tiny area with raised stools fixed to the worn lino flooring around circular tables, and a hatchway through which one could bark, 'Two bacon rolls and a coffee please, chef,' to the sweaty individual bent over a hot stove in the small galley. It was always the same request, it wasn't like there was a menu or anything, but we valued the ACRB above all other locations on the ship as the place where we could get fed at any time, day or night, when flying operations were in full swing. No need to get dressed up in order to eat, we could nip in there in our flying gear and scribble last-minute operational notes on our kneepads in wax pencil while listening to the stories from incoming aircrew who were shortly off to bed. The fabulous smell of frying bacon mixed seamlessly with other aromas: marine diesel, aviation fuel, sweaty aviators, cigarette smoke. If you pressed your nose out of the one tiny porthole you might even smell the sea.

The place we feared above all others was Flyco, the Flying Control Room, an entirely glass-sided structure that stuck out from the side of the island like an accusing finger pointing at aviators. It was a long walk from your parked aircraft to the heavy steel doorway in the side of the island that led to the bowels of the vessel and, in the event of a poor approach or landing, you took that walk in trepidation of the flight-deck tannoy booming out, 'Sub Lieutenant Grayson, report to Flyco.' This meant the bacon roll would have to wait while you presented your miserable self to Commander Air, or 'Wings' as he was universally referred to throughout the Fleet Air Arm.

Wings had a position in our lives not unlike that of God. He lived above us and was rarely glimpsed, but we walked upon his hallowed ground, his deeds were there for all to see, and his desires were handed down in tablets of stone. Wings was an aviator himself but probably hadn't flown for years. The very fact that he no longer flew was an irritant that defined his daily existence as he witnessed endless junior aviators making a hash of the simplest of manoeuvres, each of which he knew he could perform flawlessly and gracefully himself if only he weren't strapped to his damnable desk job; a job that was likely to be just the first in a series of desk jobs as he climbed the ladder of naval hierarchy.

Wings rarely spoke himself. His mouthpiece over the radio and the flight-deck tannoy was Lieutenant Commander Flying, or 'Little F'. Little F would usually be an ex-squadron commanding officer who was on his way to becoming a Wings in due course. Thus they made an awesome pair of grumpy old men in whose hands could lie one's entire military career. Or so it seemed to me as a squadron 'Jo', or (very) Junior Officer.

On joining an aircraft carrier for the first time, you were led around for the initial few hours because below decks was a maze. Left to your own devices you might be lost for ever. To give you a clue as to your whereabouts, doors, walls and rooms were marked with a series of letters and numbers that defined your position in the ship: how high or low, how far forward or aft and whether on the port or starboard side. But the best bet, at least to begin with, was to follow somebody from the flight deck to your cabin, and thence to the bar and wardroom. Once you could do that journey with confidence in both directions, you could gradually learn other routes that branched off to less imperative locations. After about a year on board the *Ark* I got brave and went to find the cobblers. This isn't another strange naval term; I do mean the men who made the shoes. The roles of cobbler and laundryman (there were no women on board in those days) were traditionally held by Chinese, over 250 of them in a crew of about 3,500. The journey took about 45 minutes following a sketch map. Eventually a door marked 'Cobblers' appeared and I poked my head in to find around twenty Chinese men sitting cross-legged on the floor and eating something out of bowls. One of them leapt to his feet and indicated that I should take my shoes and socks off. He produced a large notepad and drew around my feet and toes. He then produced an antique, dog-eared footwear catalogue and invited me to choose a style, which he scribbled in his notebook. Three days later I made the return journey to collect the finest pair of handmade cowboy boots you could possibly imagine, all for around the price of a few beers.

As officers we qualified for a cabin, unlike the seamen who shared large mess-decks and sometimes had to 'hot-bunk', whereby after they'd been on watch they would leap into the bed recently vacated by their opposite number.

At various times I shared a two-man cabin or a four-man cabin. Once, for a very short time, I had a cabin all to myself. The furniture was essentially the same no matter how many people shared: raised bed/s, chair, drawers under the bed, small writing desk and a tiny hanging closet.

My first cabin on the *Ark*, known as 'Two X-Ray Eight', almost uniquely actually had a porthole, a tiny circular window on the world built out of solid steel with inch-thick glass and huge securing hand-screws. It was a two-man cabin and I had the upper bunk. This had one big advantage and one big disadvantage. The advantage was I could lie in my 'pit' and watch the waves going past many storeys below. It gave one a tiny sense of being connected to the outside world, if only to know whether it was day or night and to have some idea of the weather conditions.

The disadvantage was that my sleeping position was just below the steel plating of the flight deck. During night-flying operations by the fixed-wing aircraft there would be several tons of F4 Phantom fighters, Buccaneer bombers or Gannet early-warning aircraft smashing on to the steel every 60 seconds or so, just inches from my skull. I soon learned to sleep through the cacophony and the ability to sleep through anything remains with me to this day. The only time I was woken by activity on deck was during a tie-down engine-run by a Phantom. Following some type of engine maintenance, one of the huge jets had been lashed to the deck with sturdy chains while the engines were started and gradually run up to full power, including igniting the after-burner. The after-burner produced a 30-foot flame of immense heat and power and generated noise of an intensity that ears cannot cope with, so the vibration through the kidneys and other internal organs conveys the sound instead. I awoke in a sweat, having already spent three days in bed after a barbaric operation to remove two wisdom teeth. The pain from the teeth, the screaming jet above me and the vibrating internal organs were frightening enough, but if anything else was needed to confirm that I had died and descended to Hades then the flames out of the porthole and the eerie purple light that was bouncing around the cabin did that job.

There was a certain comfort in having a well-established routine on a big fighting ship. We were either on our way to somewhere, taking part in practice wars, or alongside in a foreign port. Each day began with the 'Shareholders meeting': a gathering of all the aircrew to be briefed on the activities of the day. It was extremely bad form to be late for Shareholders but one of our number was genetically incapable of getting himself out of bed in the morning. His solution to the problem was to hollow out the centre of his mattress so that he could leave his bed looking made up and unoccupied while he was actually still asleep beneath the flat covers. A young pilot would be despatched to find him when the absence was noticed and always the Jo would return in the certainty that the missing officer was not in his cabin. There was always a good and fresh excuse as to why our missing man had to be somewhere else but eventually he was found out and had to serve time on some menial task in order to make amends.

While on our way from A to B, maybe outbound from Plymouth to the West Indies, Rio de Janeiro or the Mediterranean Sea, we used the time to train or to refresh ourselves as individuals in our various flying roles. Some days we might practise load-lifting using dummy loads of barrels suspended in a net; other days we might practise our normal anti-submarine role in simulated night or bad weather conditions by attaching a hood to the helmet of one of the pilots so he couldn't see out of the window and had to rely on the aircraft instruments.

You advanced quite quickly from the co-pilot's role into the captain's role, at which point there was a whole new landscape of skills and techniques to be learned in the management of the four-man crew and the use of the helicopter to achieve a pre-set series of defined tasks. All the individual crew practising led us to the point where we, as a squadron of about a dozen helicopters, could perform as one facet of the ship's weaponry during the conduct of a couple of weeks of mock war.

The aircraft carrier formed the centre of the carrier group, which might consist of anything up to twenty or thirty vessels, all assigned to very specific roles in the protection of the group overall. The most usual war scenario was to get the carrier group from one place to another without allowing the carrier to be 'sunk' by the opposing forces. Blue Force was the good guys (us) and Orange Force the opposition, formed usually by a group from another NATO country, most often the USA. The opposition would throw submarine, air and sea attacks at us and try to break through our defences. Presumably the results of all these tactics would be weighed up somewhere by a senior group of desk-bound admirals and something would be learned from it all. For our part, we just got on with the four-hour flying task assigned to us, had a bacon roll and went back to bed.

The act of getting airborne quickly and in an emergency is known as a scramble. When I later began flying Search and Rescue operations, we knew that at any point it was only a matter of time before we would be scrambled, so we practised for it. We looked upon it as an art form. Anything less than two minutes from the alert siren to the wheels leaving the ground was regarded as acceptable but we prided ourselves on achieving it in less than ninety seconds, and there would usually be a few stopwatches running in the crewroom by which compatriots could verify the achievement. Of course, their prime aim was to be able to give you a blow-by-blow account afterwards in the event that you made a complete hash of things.

My first scramble came unusually early in my career, barely three weeks after I'd joined *Ark Royal*. By day, the Wessex SAR helicopter would be the first responder to any incident near the *Ark*, but by night or over long distances the better-equipped Sea King would be despatched. Each night, therefore, a duty Sea King SAR crew would be assigned on a rotational basis, though we never expected to have to do anything other than be sober and able to get up and go with 30 minutes' notice.

I was shaken from my pit at around 2am with the words, 'Scramble to a ditched Sea King.' Few things galvanise you into action better than the knowledge that four of your drinking partners are somewhere out in the ocean, possibly fighting for their lives. I was still a very junior co-pilot at the time but I knew what was expected of me. We were soon employing the quick-start technique in the front cockpit while our observer (navigator) and aircrewman in the rear cabin flashed up the radar and scribbled down the location details from the incoming radio messages.

Launching on a night flight is always a bit of a shock. The dim lights of the ship are suddenly lost and your eyes have yet to adjust to the even dimmer red instrument lights in the cockpit. Taking off only a few minutes after being roused from sleep was an entirely new experience for me.

We set our best speed of about 110 knots towards the last known position of the 'downbird', which at that time was around 70 nautical miles from 'mother'. We learned on the way that our compadres had been sitting in a 40-foot night hover with their sonar extended into the water when one of their engines had decided to stop playing the game. The other engine had wound up to full power but this is not enough to prevent a fully loaded Sea King from descending gently to the surface of the ocean. We were in a relatively calm sea off the coast of Florida at the time so we were fairly confident of finding the helicopter with its blades still turning, and so it turned out to be.

The Sea King had a lower hull that was shaped like a boat to cope with just such an event. Although one engine was insufficient to support the helicopter in a hover by itself, it would be enough to get it airborne if the crew could achieve a forward speed of more than 15 knots by bouncing across the water. But it was a dicey manoeuvre that could never be practised until you were hit by the real thing. It was also a manoeuvre that required there to be a decent visual horizon to be carried out successfully. At 0300 in the morning it would be another couple of hours before the new dawn would begin to offer a horizon. John Anderson, the captain of the soggy Sea King, and his crew were therefore destined to 'fly' their aircraft up and down the gentle waves for the next two hours, concentrating solely on keeping the rotor blades out of the water. One kiss of the blades against the surface of the sea and their helicopter would be thrown violently on its side. So they rose and fell, rose and fell, as we circled above them and plotted the *Ark* as she steamed at top speed towards us. With 70 miles to cover it would be past dawn before she arrived.

After an hour had gone by the guys on the water were starting to get tired and a little seasick. They had done everything they could to prepare for a quick evacuation into their life raft if it should become necessary. All they had to do now was to strain their eyes in the darkness and try to make out the point at which the black sky met the black sea; their instruments were of little use in helping to keep their machine on an even keel in these conditions.

It was then that one of their fuel booster-pumps failed. In itself this wasn't a problem, but as an indicator of something more grave it was significant. Two big hatches under the nose of the Sea King formed the 'bows' of the boat-shaped hull and led to the main electrical bay of the helicopter. The fact that a normally reliable booster pump had failed was a fair indication that water was beginning to seep into the electrical bay and that other things would soon begin failing. Sure enough, another booster pump gave up the fight and was soon followed by some instrument lighting and then some facets of the flight stabilisation system. At this point it was time to admit defeat. Even if they could get the stricken helicopter airborne at first light, it would be increasingly difficult and soon impossible to fly it back on to the *Ark*.

As the mighty carrier came over the horizon and dawn began to break, Anderson and his crew were shutting down the helicopter, inflating the flotation gear and abandoning the machine. Wings decided that it would be better to collect the crew by boat than by our helicopter since they would need to attach ropes to the now abandoned Sea King. The sea boat was duly lowered and the crew were collected while the operation to try to get the *Ark* close enough to attach a crane line began. We landed our aircraft back on deck, no longer needed.

Then began an all-day exercise that proved to be excellent spectator sport. At some point during the recovery operation one of the flotation bags attached to the wheel area burst and the Sea King did a slow roll on to her back. Some hours later the divers had successfully attached a sturdy crane line to the top of the rotor head. The engineers and seamen slowly rolled the Sea King upright and then began a lift-up to the flight deck. However, there was so much water in the airframe by this stage that the weight was too much for the crane. At ten tons a Sea King is already a fair weight in itself but one that's full of water was clearly not going to be possible to lift. The order was given to one of the divers to try to drain some of the water but nobody had briefed him on how to open the doors. We were treated to the wonderful sight of a diver stabbing the side and underside of Her Majesty's property with a huge Navy-issue knife. It got the job done in the end, albeit rather slowly and ignominiously.

With water still spurting out of multiple stab wounds, like a toy being hoisted from the bath, the Sea King began the slow lift, at which point another small problem came to light. Within all squadron helicopters we carried a number of flares of different types and sizes for use in times of distress or, in the case of the

larger versions, for marking an object or point of interest in the water. The principle component of these flares is phosphorous and, as any schoolboy chemist will tell you, phosphorous burns brightly when added to water. As noted, there was rather a lot of water in the Sea King by this stage and, once the lifting process had introduced oxygen into the mix, the phosphorous did what phosphorous does: it began to burn.

Something close to panic ensued. Fire is something to be feared on a ship that's carrying a great deal of jet aviation fuel in addition to its own large reserves of marine diesel. Disconnecting the helicopter from the crane was no longer an option so firemen scattered everywhere, running out hoses and connecting them via a foam generation system. Soon the poor Sea King, only recently a proud and effective flying machine, was reduced to looking like a bedraggled Christmas cake. There was still a certain amount of smoke coming out of the windows and doors when she finally made her arrival back on deck.

The final part of the story was to last for three days. The engineering advice was that the airframe would have been written off by the total water immersion but that various parts of the electronics system might be salvageable if they could be washed in fresh water and dried out for conveyance back to the workshops in the UK. Personally I doubted that anything could truly be saved after a thorough soaking in salt water but, nevertheless, that was the decree. A large tarpaulin was set up next to the helicopter and filled with fresh water to be used as the bath.

The phosphorous had leaked all over the place so a fireman had to be permanently stationed next to the helicopter. His main task seemed to be extinguishing the smoking shoes of anybody who was working in the beast; yet another source of mirth to the casual bystanders. All other ship and flying operations had been suspended until the clean-up operation could be completed and the wreckage safely stowed down below in the hangar without fear of further fire breaking out. A small team of engineers laboured through the next night, led by a chief petty officer who had set himself the personal task of delicately removing the radar system and trying to salvage it. By sunrise the radar was out and all that remained was to give it a good fresh water bath in the little tarpaulin swimming pool.

The chief was smeared in grime and sweat as he manoeuvred himself into the doorway with the heavy item but was pleased to find a young sailor there who had just come on watch and was keen to help.

'What can I do to help, chief?'

'Here, lad, take this and go and bung it in the water,' said the chief as he went back into the cabin to retrieve his tools before going off watch, his task for the day complete. The young sailor, unaware of the swimming pool on the opposite side of the aircraft, walked to the edge of the flight deck and flung the radar over and down to the waves of the Atlantic below.

'What shall I do next, chief?' he asked as the senior guy stepped down to the flight deck.

'Give it a good rinse and dry it out, of course.'

Oooops!

The Navy is the subject of endless jokes about homosexuality. In the late 1960s the government of the UK officially decriminalised homosexuality in the civilian world at a time when the Navy and indeed the rest of the armed forces were clamping down on it with renewed vigour. Right up until the present day the military has remained very uneasy about the whole subject.

On promotion to a higher rank and being given access to more highly classified documentation, you have to undergo the ignominy of being PVed: Positively Vetted. I had to undergo this scrutiny before being given one of two keys to the nuclear depth charges hung beneath our Sea Kings. The PV involved a visit from two grey men in grey suits. One of them would try to look like he was asking about the weather as he enquired, '...and have you ever experienced a homosexual relationship of any kind?' Having satisfied their process by ticking all the boxes that confirmed you were a jolly good egg after all, they then pottered off to ask the family members, friends and colleagues that you had nominated on the form: 'Has he ever exhibited homosexual tendencies?' It was generally a good idea to warn your referees that this question would arise, in order to avoid them choking on their Earl Grey. I've often wondered whether any further checks were ever carried out on any of the questions asked during a PV or whether an Englishman's word was his bond and could therefore be taken at face value.

On average around 200 people were sacked from the Royal Navy each year for homosexuality, from a total force of around 40,000. If caught or reported in the 1970s, it was not unusual to serve a military jail sentence of five years, climbing to twenty years if you had succumbed to any form of blackmail along the way: a treasonable offence.

Australia was one of the first countries to decriminalise homosexuality in the Defence Force. The USA is only just asking itself whether the 'don't ask, don't tell' policy is an adult way of handling the subject. One of the anomalies in the UK was that if you quietly resigned you could claim no severance pay or privilege, whereas if you came out and came clean and let them kick you out, you could then claim these entitlements, often in the region of £10,000.

Although the British military lifted the ban on homosexuality in 2000, and by 2005 were taking advice from the Stonewall organisation on how to recruit and retain homosexual soldiers, sailors and airmen, there were soldiers in the British Army in 2007 still campaigning for separate, homosexual-only showers and loos, so that they, heterosexuals, wouldn't have to suffer the distress of baring themselves in front of 'queers'. When you've been brought up on a diet of the 1960s *Carry On* films with nudge-nudge wink-wink innuendo and all the flamboyant characters being greeted with 'Hello, sailor', it can be hard to be politically correct.

The only time I had to face my own inner homophobe was during my first tour on *Ark Royal*. Replenishing the supplies for a large aircraft carrier with around 3,500 men on board is, as you might imagine, a regular occurrence. Two other ships were usually involved, an 'oiler' for the marine diesel and the jet fuel, and another for everything else in the way of food, spare parts, ammunition and general consumables.

The process of transferring all this gear is known as a RAS, Replenishment At Sea, which is used as a verb, to ras. When rasing from an oiler, both vessels would steam on a steady heading at a speed of 12 to 16 knots, side by side. For the seamen officers who drove the ships it was a skilled and precise operation. Too far apart and the hoses wouldn't reach; too close and the Venturi effect would suck both ships together, causing a great deal of damage to both. The standard distance was around 30 metres.

Once this formation had been accurately established, gun lines would be fired from one ship to another. Each gun line would then be hauled back, bringing a stronger 'messenger line' with it. Then the messenger line would be pulled back in order to bring across the transfer rig, a telephone line and a distance line with bright markers. Sometimes this would be happening in up to four locations along the side of the carrier to accelerate the whole process. Oilers such as RFA *Olna*, *Olwen* and *Olmeda* would often block out the sunshine from a Caribbean dawn as they steamed alongside.

The Royal Fleet Auxiliary vessels with dry stores were RFA *Reliant*, *Resource* and *Regent*. In the later Falklands War it was RFA *Resource* that took up the task of recovering survivors and bodies from HMS *Sheffield* when she was hit by an Exocet missile and burned. *Resource* had only just finished replenishing *Sheffield* a short time earlier. (In an episode entirely typical of the wonderfully absurd world of a naval officer, the survivors of *Sheffield*, while awaiting rescue, were led by Sub Lieutenant Carrington-Wood in singing the Monty Python song 'Always Look on the Bright Side of Life'. They still sing it at reunions to this day.)

The process for transferring dry stores was much the same except that instead of the thick, black, rubber oil lines, a constant stream of heavily loaded pallets would be pulled across. If there was a need for personnel transfer, a little red cage would travel across the 12-knot ravine while the hapless occupant bounced up and down on the wire.

In view of the time it took to complete this process, and the fact that it precluded fixed-wing flying operations, a carrier would often ras from an oiler on one side and a dry supply vessel on the other. The process could then be further accelerated by using a helicopter to sling pallets from one flight deck to the other. One horrifying incident involved one of the ground crew getting his foot stuck in the net beneath the helicopter and being flown from one ship to another suspended only by his ankle. Vertical replenishment by helicopter (VERTREP) was sometimes the only way in which the barest minimum of supplies could be transferred, such as when the sea state was too rough for the vessels to steam safely alongside each other. The RFA would then formate a few hundred yards away and one, two or sometimes three helicopters would fly a continuous pattern of loads from supplier to customer.

Part way through one of these rasing operations, the ships had to separate and go in opposite directions. The idea was that we would continue to extend the length of each flight until finally it became too far to continue, at which point we would land on *Ark Royal* and discontinue. Sadly this didn't quite work out, through a combination of bad weather and confusion by senior officers, with the result that my aircraft ended up having to shut down on the back of the RFA.

This interlude allowed us to grab a bite of lunch with the RFA officers and then, as the length of our stay increased, even take a

tour of the ship. Let me tell you that I finally had my eyes opened and found out where 'Hello, sailor' had originated.

Although owned by the Ministry of Defence, the RFA organisation is manned by civilian sailors. Somehow it had become the employment of choice for gay seamen back in the 1960s. This small fact was so obvious to the officer showing us around that he didn't bother commenting on it. I was a bit perplexed when the first wolf whistle rang out, but by the time we'd passed the open door to a few of the living quarters my eyes were out on stalks. Sumptuous purple curtains were the first clue, but a glance inside affirmed that the décor would have been regarded as garish in a Bangkok brothel, complete with double beds. Approaching a better-lit area I began to realise that all the sailors were wearing heavy makeup and I started to feel uncomfortable at the stares my co-pilot and I were getting from couples standing idly with their arms around each other.

I hasten to add that I have no idea whether this was a feature of the RFA in general or a temporary feature of a specific ship at a time long before such sights would become more commonplace in communities ashore. Nevertheless, when a small window of weather opportunity showed up, we had our engines started and rotors turning more quickly than if our lives had depended on it. Rarely was I more relieved to land back on the mighty *Ark* and to know that I'd be spending the night in my own small cabin, even if it did only have one small piece of grey cloth to keep the light out.

Two years after leaving *Ark Royal* I found myself back on the ship in the full-time rescue role, rather than in the anti-submarine role of the Sea Kings. The *Ark* carried two very old Wessex Mark 1 rescue helicopters and I was one of only a handful of pilots qualified to fly them. I had been scheduled to take some leave from my shore-based SAR duties at that time. My wife and I had booked a holiday in Amsterdam and I had sent my passport away for renewal. When one of the three SAR

pilots on the *Ark* had to be evacuated for a severe medical problem it fell to me to replace him, but at that time the carrier was in mid-Atlantic and I was therefore despatched from my base at Culdrose to Lisbon to await further instructions. The holiday was cancelled and, not having a passport, I was issued with a scruffy single sheet of paper called a 'NATO travel warrant'. This, as you might imagine, took a lot of explaining at the various customs points en route.

I reached Lisbon, presented myself to the British Embassy as instructed, and retired to the hotel I had been allocated just down the road. Twenty-four hours later a messenger arrived with a ticket for a commercial flight leaving for one of the islands of the Azores the next morning, and the instruction that I would be met there. Few places on earth are quite as remote as these Portuguese islands, lying nearly halfway across the North Atlantic towards Canada.

After a couple of hours we touched down at an airfield surrounded by scrub land and I disembarked along with only one other passenger, a young lady who was promptly whisked away into the bosom of her overjoyed family. The guy who had provided the stairs to the small airliner then got into a clapped-out station wagon and drove off, leaving me standing with a small bag on a vast airfield of weed-covered concrete with not another soul in sight. There was nothing recognisable as an airport infrastructure and the airliner was already rolling down the runway, presumably on its way back to Portugal. It hadn't even paused long enough to stop the engines.

Crickets were chirping and a gentle warm breeze blowing as I stood there wondering what on earth I was expected to do next. I set about exploring the dilapidated huts next to the apron and they all seemed to indicate that this had once been an American airbase, but obviously many years earlier. I set off down the dirt track in the direction I'd seen the cars go but after a mile with still no sign of life it occurred to me that whoever I was supposed to be met by might arrive, find me gone, and disappear, so I retraced my steps.

Just as I was about to begin a proper audit of the deserted encampment of huts with a view to beginning some form of survival exercise for an indeterminate period, the wonderful sound of a Sea King could be heard faintly in the distance. Sure enough, one of my old squadron machines arrived in a cloud of dust, the door flew open and an aircrewman I knew only slightly beckoned me over. 'Sorry we're a bit late,' he shouted as he clamped a set of ear defenders on my head and off we went across the ocean. Two hours later the chockheads were clamping us down to the familiar deck of the mighty *Ark*.

Being on the *Ark* as the SAR pilot turned out to be a very different experience from being there as a junior anti-submarine pilot, or 'Pinger', as I had previously been known. Pingers were regarded with disdain by the fighter pilots or 'Stovies'. (Why Stovies? Because their jets looked like stove pipes, of course.) The SAR pilot, on the other hand, was the guy who would fetch them out of the water when it all turned to rats, so he was not only included in wardroom conversation but was frequently rewarded with drinks.

I totally, absolutely, loved the role. Prior to the start of fixed-wing operations, the SAR Wessex would wind up, get airborne and position herself just off the port side of the carrier. There she would sit, guarding over the successful launch and recovery of every fixed-wing flight; hence the official role name of 'Planeguard'. It was the best seat in the house for one of the most dramatic shows you could ever hope to see.

First the fighters and bombers would start their engines, a cacophony of sound I could readily hear despite being airborne in a helicopter with a helmet on. The first would then taxi forward under the crisply waved instructions of one marshaller after another until it arrived at the Cat, a steam-driven catapult that was about to accelerate the jet up to over 100 knots in only a few yards. With practised precision a small crew in brightly coloured vests would throw themselves under the aircraft, attach a massive metal strop to the underside by hooks and then attach the same strop to the heavy metal shoe of the catapult. The yellow-vested Flight Deck Officer (FDO) would indicate for the Cat to take up the slack, at which point the jet's nose would rise until it looked like a crouching tiger ready to spring. As the FDO began waving his flag vigorously in a circular motion above his head the jet would wind up to full throttle, then light the afterburner. We could barely talk to each other in the hovering helicopter as the brutal force permeated our helmets and eardrums. The FDO glanced first at the jet pilot for a thumbs-up, then looked ahead of the ship to time the launch as the bows of the carrier were rising over the next swell. As he dropped his flag to the deck, the combined power of the Cat and the fully powered jet engine combined to throw the jet off the front of the flight deck. This was always a heart-stopping moment, and was the reason for the SAR helicopter.

Even with all that power a Cat launch would only just get these heavy jets up to flying speed, so it was normal to see them fly flat for the first mile ahead of the ship until they had accelerated enough to climb. If they were particularly heavy or if the FDO mis-timed the rise and fall of the carrier bows, it was not unusual to see a Phantom drop closer to the sea before beginning to climb. In days gone by many aircraft were lost this way. Originally the procedure in that event was for the ship to turn as sharply as it could away from the ditched aircraft while the SAR helicopter leapt forward to retrieve the crew, but that all changed in the mid-1960s when a carrier ran over both the aircraft in the water and the helicopter in the air, with the loss of both crews. By my time on the *Ark* the procedure was that the crew of the fixed wing should stay in their aircraft and allow the ship to run over the top of them as they sank. Once the four propellers had passed over them they should then explosively release the canopy and come to the surface where the SAR would pick them out of the water. Rod O'Connor, an observer who had flown many hours in the back seat of various jets, claimed to have seen the entire underside of a carrier on four separate occasions. Thankfully this was not a procedure I ever witnessed or had to participate in during either of my tours on the *Ark*.

To launch the fixed wing, the carrier would always turn into wind; just a few extra knots of wind across the deck could make all the difference. But this often meant that the ship was travelling on an opposite course from the direction in which she wanted to be travelling. Therefore, as soon as the last aircraft had been launched, the ship would execute an enormous turn, leaving the SAR pilot to struggle with landing on a flight deck that was heeled heavily over to one side, constantly changing direction and rapidly facing out of the wind. It always resulted in a race to get back on deck.

There was time for a quick bacon roll before the call 'hands to recovery stations' in preparation for the return of the jets. We once again resumed our Planeguard position for an even more awesome procedure than the catapult launches. A Phantom or a Buccaneer couldn't fly much slower than 100 knots before falling out of the sky and if it were to land successfully then it had to be decelerated to a stop in the available 400 feet or so. To do this the flight deck had four massive wires stretched out across it. Numbered from 1 to 4, it was generally number 3 wire that the pilots were hoping to catch with the hook they lowered from the tail during their approach to the deck. Each wire was attached to a pair of cylinders that ran almost the entire length of the ship beneath the flight deck. The action of the pistons in the cylinders, compressing the air within them, caused the eye-popping deceleration of the big jets. After each landing the cylinder would be reset and the wire checked for damage. If it was damaged, there was no time for replacement. It had to be cut with oversized hydraulic bolt croppers and laid to one side of the 'runway'. Better to have one less wire available than for a jet to catch one that broke part-way through deceleration.

Trying to land 27,000 kilograms of supersonic Phantom jet on the tiny deck of a ship that is rising and falling on an often rough ocean takes a peculiar type of skill. Pilots were constantly assessed and graded according to their abilities. The newbies would only be allowed to fly if there was a suitable diversion airfield available on land nearby and they carried sufficient fuel to reach it. The real aces were allowed to fly without that safety net, and often by night.

Each aircraft would arrive overhead at about 1,000 feet and descend into a left-hand pattern in order to line up with the flight deck. The final mile was judged visually by a complex lighting arrangement known as the 'meatball', and aurally by barked instructions over the radio from a highly skilled and experienced Landing Sight Officer. You could hear the enormous power changes being made during the final stage of the approach as the pilot tried to judge it just right to catch one of the wires. If they failed to catch any of the four wires they would be committed to a 'bolter', whereby they bounced off the deck and had to resume flying speed before dropping off the edge. With so little time to react, the pilots were trained to apply full power even before they knew whether they had caught a wire or not. Failure to apply enough power sufficiently early would result in a 'whispering bolter': the jet would flutter over the end of the flight deck towards the sea and everybody would hold their breath until it reappeared above the horizon gaining speed and climbing.

After a successful approach and landing, the wire would be given some slack and would fall automatically off the arrester hook, allowing the aircraft to taxi forward to a parking spot in the catapult area on the bows. The most feared result was an aircraft approaching too low and catching the rounded edge of the deck before ever reaching the wires. An aircraft crashing into the stern of the ship could easily cause the total loss of the carrier in the ensuing fire. At some point in their careers all pilots are shown the horrifying video of a fire on board the USS *Forrestal*, an American aircraft carrier on which a weapon was inadvertently fired from one parked aircraft into another, sparking a sequence of explosions which resulted in 134 deaths, and nearly in the loss of the ship altogether.

One of the great characters on the *Ark* was Phantom pilot 'Wiggy' Bennett. He was approaching to land one night when he was struck by a vortex of turbulence coming off the ship. His aircraft turned upside down and he managed an extraordinary job in both righting the aircraft and executing a successful landing. When he woke up the next morning every hair on his head lay loose on the pillow, leaving him completely bald, presumably from the shock of the near miss. His nickname came from the fact that the Navy issued him with two wigs: one for time on duty and one, slightly longer, for time ashore.

The only near catastrophe I witnessed with fixed wing on the *Ark* was a bolter by a Fairey Gannet. This was a bizarre flying machine, first introduced in 1953 but still in service in the late 1970s. Like all carrier aircraft it had folding wings to fit it in the hangar below decks, but the weird propulsion system was achieved by two engines lying side by side in the nose driving its two contra-rotating propellers. A Gannet returning from a long-range flight one afternoon had tried to jettison the long-range fuel tanks carried beneath the wings but only one had dropped. The other one was still hanging there but, of course, there was no way of knowing how securely. It was a nice approach but the aircraft missed all four wires and, as she hit the deck and commenced the bolter, the remaining empty fuel tank came off, bounced back up from the flight deck and took away part of the tail-plane. The pilot did a great job in wrestling his aircraft round another circuit and making a faultless landing second time around.

Far too quickly, or so it seemed to me, the SAR pilot I had replaced returned to duty and I left *Ark Royal* for the final time in order to continue my shore time as a rescue pilot. She was a magnificent ship and I have only happy memories of my life on board. She was replaced by a much smaller aircraft carrier and even that has just been retired as I write this.

ADMIRALS

I HAVEN'T MET AN ADMIRAL, serving or retired, since I was in my twenties. Even today, I think of an admiral as being of such immense seniority and superiority that he must be woven from a different fabric from the rest of us. As a lowly lieutenant you are sufficiently in awe of a commander to chop off a smart salute as he approaches and to stand to attention if he should speak, but a commander only represents two tiers of managerial level above your own. You can imagine, therefore, that an admiral is some kind of deity.

An admiral has gold rings around his cuffs, and his long-brimmed cap bears a latticework of leaves fashioned from fine gold thread. He is driven around in a long black car with triangular flags fluttering from the bonnet, denoting his position in the megalithic organisation he runs. These lofty positions have acronyms such as FONAC (Flag Officer Naval Air Command) and FOCAS (Flag Officer Carriers and Amphibious Ships). Pyramids of staff bustle around behind admirals, hanging on their every word and jumping to ensure the slightest request is fulfilled immediately and completely. At the top of this pyramid sits the most senior assistant, usually a lieutenant commander known by the acronym ADC (Aide-de-Campe), effectively a chief of staff. The ADC gets to wear a rope of gold from his uniform, denoting the importance of his station.

The role of admiral in all seafaring nations carries with it centuries of tradition and entitlement. One of their entitlements is to a dedicated Admiral's Barge, a smartly appointed motor boat to convey them to and from their flagship. Its paintwork gleams and its brass fittings are polished to a diamond shine. Smart sailors in heavily starched uniforms move as clockwork during the departure and arrival procedure of the barge, always preceded by the blowing of pipes to herald the movement of the admiral. In such grandeur, an admiral travels ashore to his embassy cocktail parties. By contrast, the sailors travel ashore to their drinking haunts in a 'liberty boat', not much more than a large wooden lifeboat.

When the flagship, usually an aircraft carrier or similarly large warship, is too big to go alongside at the destination port it will often drop anchor in a sheltered bay or inlet nearby. We did this several times during my tour of duty on the *Ark Royal*. I particularly remember being anchored off Rio de Janeiro with the twinkling lights of the city across the water and the huge and inspiring mountainous backdrop, including the famous Sugar Loaf. To reach these twinkling lights the sailors had to join a long queue of their colleagues, similarly desperate for the delights of a city after several weeks at sea, all waiting for the next liberty boat. The liberty boat on the outbound trip was always full of happy faces lit up with anticipation. Returning liberty boats were an entirely different story, full of dishevelled sailors, their heads drooping from exhaustion and alcohol.

Each destination, of course, had its own character and its own associated routine for a run ashore. In the warmer, more exotic countries this would sometimes feature a 'banyan': a squadron barbecue, sports extravaganza and general binge on the beach. During a particularly pleasant voyage around the Caribbean the *Ark Royal* anchored several miles out from the island of Barbados. A skeleton crew stayed on board to run the ship while the rest of us clambered into the liberty boats for our run of R&R ashore. In Barbados the drink of preference was Bacardi and Coke. You could take a large plastic water bottle into just about any shop on the island and fill it with the clear nectar for a pittance. With a slab of Coke and a bag of ice you were equipped for the beach.

When the sun went down on Barbados that night we retired to the dimly lit hot spots of the old town and tried fruitlessly to drink the island dry. I woke up the next day, Easter Sunday, on the wrong end of the island with no public transport to take me back to the port. My feet were in rags by the time I arrived back at the port around eight in the evening and the liberty boats leaving were packed. I couldn't be bothered to wait for an officers' boat and so I squeezed in with three hundred sailors, most of whom might have failed in their attempt to drink the island dry but had given it a good shot. With the lights of the *Ark* growing gradually more distinct, a tranquil sea and a pretty pink hue on the horizon, I was just daring to dream about soaking my poor feet in a bucket of cold water. Unfortunately a big splash just at that moment signalled the unscheduled departure of one of our number into the warm waters of the Caribbean. Full of bravado and enthusiasm the other 299 sailors shouted, 'I'll get him, sir!' and hurled themselves into the sea to rescue their compatriot. It was many hours later before we'd collected everybody and made our way back to the mighty *Ark*, by which time the desperate need for sleep had overwhelmed any lingering desire for a foot bath. Such are the joys of the liberty boat. But I digress.

There was also a flying version of the Admiral's Barge, known as a Green Parrot. A couple of these bizarrely painted light-green

Wessex V helicopters were based at Portland. They were used to ferry admirals to and from the warships to the south, all of whom were engaged in the 'Thursday War' exercise, where they test their fighting skills against each other. Towards the end of his Navy flying career, an old mate from our flying training days together, Mike Briggs, was assigned to the task of driving admirals around in the Green Parrot. There wasn't a lot you could do to the interior cabin of a Wessex V (Mark 5) to make it suitable for an admiral, but a half-hearted attempt was made by using white canvas for seating instead of the usual drab and oil-covered blue.

I must first explain a small technical point. The Wessex V had two engines meshed to the rotors via a huge gearbox. The cockpit was therefore pretty full of instruments showing the state of play in the two engines, the gearbox, the dual hydraulic systems, and a multitude of other moving parts. To facilitate easy appreciation of whether all was as it should be, the instruments were rotated in the panel such that in the normal operating state all the needles pointed upwards. In this way a quick glance at over twenty gauges would soon alert the pilot to anything amiss and, assuming there wasn't, he could confidently and quickly transfer his eyes back to the outside of the helicopter. There was also an array of warning lights, each of which would illuminate if its associated system ran above, or fell below, the predetermined safe parameters. But the problem was that they often malfunctioned, or at least gave spurious warnings, so we had to take them seriously but also with a certain amount of scepticism. On occasions you might see, for example, a gradually increasing engine temperature but you wouldn't worry too much about it until and unless you saw a secondary indication, such as falling oil pressure on the same engine. At that point you knew you had a serious situation developing and needed to put the emergency (or at least precautionary) checklist into action.

One fine afternoon Mike was on his way north to Portland from the exercise to the south. Aboard his Green Parrot were, besides his crewman down in the cabin, an admiral and his ADC. Still several miles out from the airbase Mike began to notice a declining oil pressure in the main gearbox, which he mentioned on the intercom to his crewman. The admiral and the ADC were none the wiser, having elected at the start of the trip to don only the lighter ear defenders and not a full headset with mics.

A few miles further on the temperature in the gearbox began to rise: the dreaded secondary indication. A seized gearbox on a helicopter means the rotors stop turning and the only direction of travel then available is down. So Mike did entirely the right thing and prepared to ditch his aircraft into the English Channel. He discussed the situation with his crewman, who brought the inflatable life raft to the door of the cabin. Mike briefed the crewman that the two passengers should be 'egressed' first, at which point he would hover the aircraft a good distance away before ditching it in the water. In this way the admiral and the ADC would be spared the extra difficulty of having to escape from a sinking helicopter.

The theory is that in a light sea state you can inflate the flotation bags attached to the wheels, land on the water, stop the rotors and step gently into the life raft your crewman has politely inflated. But as aircrew we all train in 'the Dunker', a horrible contraption that simulates the cockpit and cabin of a helicopter as it sinks beneath the waves. You are taught to strap in tight, take a deep breath and remain secured until everything is flooded and the aircraft has stopped revolving. In this way you avoid being disorientated and can more easily find the exit point in the dark as she sinks. A helicopter is much heavier at the top than at the bottom so it will almost certainly roll on to its back as it begins its journey to the sea bed. The procedure does work and, although I've been lucky enough never to have to try it out for real, it is said by those who have that the training was invaluable but that it is still unbelievably frightening.

So, Mike came to a low hover, the crewman unstrapped himself and in a series of deft movements he relieved the (still unaware) admiral of his copy of *The Times* newspaper, unstrapped him and hurled him out of the open doorway of the helicopter into the sea below. At this point the ADC took umbrage at his boss being so unceremoniously ejected from the flight and Mike became aware of a punch-up breaking out between crewman and ADC in the cabin beneath him. Inevitably an officer used to spending his days pushing paper across the admiral's desk was no match for the bulk of a finely honed crewman who runs across mud flats for sport, and the ADC was soon wrestled out of the door to make a big splash next to the Flag Officer, who had thankfully found the ring-pull on his life jacket. The crewman then diligently hurled the life raft into the water beside them and Mike hovered the aircraft a good half mile away to be sure of not injuring his floating passengers.

But then a funny thing happened. In the process of hovering away Mike noticed that the temperature on the gearbox began to come back towards normal, as did the pressure. Mike told the crewman that it was possible the hover attitude, in other words the changed angle at which the helicopter hangs from the rotors, had increased the opportunity for the oil to flow through to the cooler. He therefore announced his intention to try to hover his way back to the airfield, only a couple of miles away. Sure enough, as he nursed the stricken craft back towards the shore he was able to keep his instruments 'in the green' by simply remaining in a drifting hover and not tipping the nose of the aircraft down to accelerate to forward flight. Eventually the concrete of the runway appeared beneath them and Mike was able to land normally and shut down his aircraft, just as a second helicopter took off from the other end of the runway to retrieve the soggy admiral and staff.

It's an odd thing that they never did find anything wrong with that gearbox and there are no recording devices to bear witness to the events as told. But Mike was able to conclude his naval flying career, which by an extraordinary coincidence was scheduled to happen the very next day, without losing his aircraft. Try as we might, we could never get him to admit to the wonderful parting shot he appeared to have pulled off so flawlessly.

SUBMARINES

A SUBMARINE HAS TO BE ONE OF mankind's most terrifying inventions, both for those within it and for those who encounter one. It is nothing more than a finely developed killing machine, and a truly enormous one at that. The Soviet Union has built the biggest ever seen, the 'Shark' class as it was named by the Russians, or the 'Typhoon' class as it was known by NATO. The six boats (a submarine is always known as a 'boat', not a ship) in the class were introduced into the latter stages of the Cold War in the 1980s but have since been decommissioned and had their teeth removed as part of the remarkable deal brokered and agreed by Gorbachev, Thatcher and Reagan. Whatever your politics you have to admire their guts and their vision; truly brave and innovative leaders don't come along very often. The Typhoon was 574 feet long and displaced 48,000 tons. That's the length of ten train carriages – all underwater, of course.

I'm slightly inaccurate in saying that the six were decommissioned, as one of them, the *Kursk*, made worldwide headlines in August 2000 when she sank in the Barents Sea with the loss of 118 lives. Officially she suffered an accident when a torpedo exploded within her, but this is one of those stories surrounded by conspiracy theories and dark mutterings, as so often seems to happen when talking about the most secret of machines that any navy operates.

These huge boats, just like those of their American opposition, carried multiple ballistic missiles, each of which could deliver multiple warheads to multiple destinations. As a military strategy it was known as Mutually Assured Destruction or MAD. Never has there been a more apt acronym. The theory goes that if you're both so comprehensively armed to the teeth that each can entirely destroy the homeland of the other then neither of you will ever be stupid enough to press the button.

Broadly two types of submarine are in use today: the Boomers, which carry the MAD doomsday weapons, and the attack submarines, which prowl the seas looking for each other, for Boomers or for surface ships. Torpedoes are the usual weapon by which attack submarines achieve their destruction: great long cigars of metal packed with high explosives. A torpedo today looks entirely similar to one from the Second World War but it's much more cunning inside. The wartime 'fish', as a torpedo is known, simply travelled as fast as possible in a single direction until it either hit something or ran out of the battery power that drove its little propeller. Today's fish can be pre-programmed to perform in many diverse ways. They can execute complex search patterns in three dimensions and they carry sensors of their own which will then alter the search pattern to suit the circumstances they find themselves in. Of all military subjects it is the exact capabilities of subs and their fish that carry the highest security classification. I must therefore shy away from going into any more detail.

Submarines are either nuclear-powered or use diesel/electric. The nukes have a small reactor in the bowels that provides all the power, light, heat and desalinated water facilities they need. Some other form of magic also generates oxygen. Nuclear-powered boats can stay submerged for enormous amounts of time; I'm not even sure if there's a limit. The big Boomers, the nuclear-powered submarines that also carry nuclear missiles, depart their home port, submerge and stay that way for several months. They might completely circumnavigate the globe in that time or they may position to a particular area and just loiter. Very few people on the boat know where they are or where they've been; it's a closely guarded secret that leads sailors to return home after several months at sea with no suntan, no presents from far-flung lands and no idea of where their voyage has taken them. Facilities on submarines, particularly on diesel/electric boats, are cramped and limited, which is why submariners tend to have a certain odour about them.

The older and smaller submarines are powered by diesel/electric. On the surface they will be propelled by their diesel engines, which are simultaneously powering a generator to charge the batteries. But of course a diesel engine requires air to run on, so as soon as the submarine dives it must switch to electric power. Actually, that's slightly inaccurate: they can sit just beneath the surface and extend a snorkel, next to the periscope, to allow the diesel engines to run. With fully charged batteries they can run silent and deep until, like a whale, they must eventually come up for air again. In the anti-submarine role we learned to tune our eyes for the faintest sign of what might be a wake from a periscope or a snorkel, since this is when a submarine is at its most vulnerable.

During my time on HMS *Ark Royal* and HMS *Hermes* our prime role in the Sea Kings was anti-submarine. This often involved a particularly unpleasant routine – unpleasant for its effects on the body clock – known as 'Ripple three', which consisted of keeping three aircraft airborne continuously for up to ten days and 'rippling' the aircrews so that they changed over every four hours when the helicopter had to return to 'mother' for fuel. To fit in with this routine we would work six hours on, six hours off, six hours on, six hours off… for what felt like for ever. Very few cabins had any view of the outside world and you always rose in darkness in order not to disturb the others, who were inevitably at some point in the sleep cycle. Towards the end of a ten-day ripple you would struggle to interpret the faintly illuminated hands of the clock. On a couple of occasions I simply couldn't resolve the issue of whether it was day or night until I finally stepped out on the flight deck or caught a glimpse of the outside world en route to the flight briefing room.

On one particularly rough exercise, Ocean Safari in the North Sea just off Norway, I passed one of the ship's officers on my way to the briefing room. He'd just come off watch in the operations room. 'You'd better go and look at the radar. You won't believe your eyes.' There was an unusual fervour in the normally placid ops room as I slid open the door to the darkened space and craned my neck over the crowd gathered around the long-range radar. There were so many airborne contacts on the screen it looked as though it was snowing, or perhaps as if someone were playing the Space Invaders game that would follow some years later. With each sweep of the radar beam the snowstorm advanced a little further in our direction. I didn't have to hang around very long to overhear that we were looking at a huge number of Russian 'Bear' bombers flooding from their Motherland into the Baltic Sea. For some considerable time, although none of us dared voice our fears, we believed we might be looking first hand at the prelude to a Third World War. Icicles gripped my spine and a true realisation of the job we'd signed on for began to dawn on us all. After a couple of hours the multiple contacts simply turned around and headed back into the heart of the Soviet Union. It became an assumption on board that we'd simply witnessed a classic show of military force from the mighty superpower in response to our exercise and, although it was out of all usual proportions, the incident was forgotten.

Some twenty-five years later I was watching a documentary about the real story behind *The Hunt For Red October*, a great novel by Tom Clancy that was turned into an equally great movie starring Sean Connery and Alec Baldwin. As I learned from the documentary, Clancy's story of a submarine captain who mutinies and takes his vessel into the hands of the USA had its genesis in a real incident on 9 November 1975 when Captain Valery Sablin of the Soviet frigate *Storozhevoy* set out from Riga in Latvia without authorisation in order to broadcast a message of protest against the rampant corruption in the Soviet leadership. Brezhnev was roused from his bed and ordered the frigate to be stopped at all costs. Initially the pilots refused to fire on their comrades but eventually bombs were dropped around the vessel, the crew surrendered and Captain Sablin and twenty-six others were summarily executed a few weeks later. The date rang a bell and a quick check in my logbook confirmed that this was indeed the horrifying story I'd been watching unfold on the ship's radar all those years earlier.

Our task in the anti-submarine role was to prevent submarines from getting close enough to the convoy, and to our own aircraft carrier, to fire on us with their torpedoes. The task of the 'enemy', the NATO submarine commanders in the exercise, was of course to slip past us. On a couple of occasions the top submariners not only evaded our search blanket but also took up position beneath the carrier and had photographs of the keel to prove the point. The Russians knew exactly where and when we were exercising and often pitted themselves against us to learn more about our capabilities (or lack thereof). We always knew when they were taking an interest in us because a thinly disguised Russian 'fishing boat' would take up position behind our carrier and could be seen collecting and sifting through the rubbish bags we discarded overboard. We had to be careful what we threw away, warned in training videos that the tiniest personal detail could be used as blackmail leverage. Our preventative task was boring for 99 per cent of the time but once contact was made with a submarine it did become an exciting game of cat and mouse.

I only once went head to head with a Russian submarine captain and it was undoubtedly one of the most exciting hours of flying I ever spent in the Sea King. We dropped into a 40-foot hover over the ocean and lowered the sonar transducer into the water by means of a big hydraulic winch cable. The sonar operator first listened intently, then sent out a couple of active sonar pings to try to establish the position of the sub. Alerted to our presence, the sub captain tried the first of the many evasive manoeuvres we were to see him perform over the next hour. Sometimes he would sit silently and hope we couldn't find him; other times he would try to outrun us. He would dive deep, put out decoys or bubbles of air, or take refuge in a layer of water that was at a different temperature and would therefore deflect the soundwaves travelling from our active sonar. At certain moments we would try to jump much closer to where we judged his position to be. We would rapidly raise the sonar transducer into the body of the helicopter from 300 feet beneath the waves, apply full power and accelerate to the new position. We'd arrive in a flurry of saltwater downwash and hastily lower the sonar equipment. Time and again we repeated this, often remaining in the hover for only a few seconds. The Russian captain could usually hear us and therefore judge his moment to change tactics from fast and noisy to silent and deep, or vice versa. Skill pitted against skill, and all with the 'real enemy' instead of a friendly simulation. My four-man crew loved every minute of it, but it was a rare event indeed.

Our lords and masters took these war games pretty seriously; we were, after all, supposed to be defending the realm and the last glorious remnants of the British Empire. For those of us at the coal face, we had joined for a life of adventure and the opportunity of flight training and operational experience that was unsurpassed anywhere in the world. We took the aviation extremely seriously, but the war game stuff was only of importance to the guys who'd decided on an entire career in the Navy and were busy climbing the ladder of authority. Alongside the sonar operator in the rear of the Sea King, our observer was usually the grown-up of the crew. It was often his task to take charge of several surface assets (ships, to you and me) as the complicated game of chess played out. On one particularly dark night in the Mediterranean the plan was that the carrier task group, consisting of our 'mother' and about another twenty warships, would try to evade detection and sneak out into the Atlantic. Somebody had come up with the genius plan to decorate all the warships in glittering arrays of light strings, so that they would from a distance appear to be cruise ships.

With my mate Bob Fewings as the observer and aircraft captain, we took off and headed east into the Med to protect the convoy from submarines. The brief was that we should maintain complete radio silence in a further attempt to evade detection. The bright wands of the deck marshaller were the last sign of humanity we would see for a while as we launched into an inky black night over an equally black sea. After an hour we were to climb high and reverse our direction to the west, pass high overhead and begin to sweep the Atlantic beyond Gibraltar. In the meantime the convoy would also reverse course and head for the open ocean with all their pretty lights ablaze. In this way, so the theory went, the 'enemy' would see that the force was initially headed into the Med and would therefore take little notice of departing cruise ships later in the night.

The first hour was rather dull, dark and tedious, but at the allotted time we raised our sonar, climbed to 5,000 feet and headed out through the gap towards the Atlantic. From our lofty height the sparkies had done a wonderful job and as we briefly glimpsed the *Ark* through a gap in the clouds my co-pilot, Terry Jane, and I remarked on how much she did indeed look like a cruise ship. Bob kept close watch on the continuing progress of the *Ark* as she steamed in our direction, while we pinged our way along looking for submarines. Constantly updating the speed/time/distance/fuel calculations, he was carefully picking the moment at which we would have to depart our task and run for Mother. We timed it to perfection, continued to exercise the discipline of complete radio silence, and began our final approach to the aircraft carrier. It was with dawning horror that we realised the vessel we'd flown over had indeed been a cruise ship and as we came alongside her it was apparent that she had no space whatsoever to accommodate a large and thirsty helicopter.

Not another vessel showed on the radar for many miles around and, as we would later discover, the carrier convoy had never actually made the turn to the west and were now at least two hundred miles back inside the Mediterranean Sea. An emergency diversion to Gibraltar was our only option and we set off in that direction at the speed that would best preserve our dwindling fuel supply. While I put out a 'Pan' call, which is a code word used with Air Traffic Control to indicate that you have a problem but not one that warrants the more serious 'Mayday', and declared our intention to divert to the airport at Gibraltar, we made all the usual preparations for landing in the water if that should become necessary. The four of us were continually calculating and recalculating the remaining fuel and distance and were all arriving at the same conclusion: provided the wind did not change, we had a 50/50 chance of making it to dry land.

At the height of diplomatic tensions concerning ownership of this bizarre outpost of British supremacy (Spain closed its land border with Gibraltar in 1969 and it was fully opened again only sixteen years later), the approach to the airport was by no means simple. Buoys in the bay marked the boundary between the airspaces belonging to Spain and to England. You crossed that line of buoys at your peril, and in the knowledge that it would almost certainly spark some sort of international incident involving paperwork and infamy. The lights of the town nestled beneath the mighty Rock seemed to grow in the windscreen only very slowly indeed. We found the buoy that marked the first turning point at the edge of Spanish airspace and turned north and into the bay extremely gingerly. By now the fuel gauges were showing way below the legal minimum and both 'Fuel Low' lights were starting to flash at us persistently. Anything more than the gentlest of turns ran the serious risk of washing the fuel to one side of the tank and exposing the fuel feed line to nothing but air. The second turning point came into view and we executed another very tenuous turn in the opposite direction to line up with the runway, which bisected the narrow junction between Gibraltar and Spain. It was so narrow that the main road ran across the runway and the traffic had to be stopped by lights each time the runway was used. But at three o'clock in the morning most sensible inhabitants were fast asleep and we were able to continue our approach without hindrance. We dared not flare to a hover – pull the helicopter nose up to decelerate quickly – for just the same reason we had performed such gentle turns, so we committed ourselves to a running landing and were highly relieved to cross the runway threshold and settle gently on to the concrete with two engines still running. My logbook confirms 4 hours 30 minutes of night flying in a helicopter that should only fly for four hours.

On just one occasion in my anti-submarine career we carried a nuclear weapon. It was only as an exercise but was no less terrifying for that. It used to be a state secret that our Sea Kings were capable of carrying nuclear depth charges, but it became public knowledge

when an MP accidentally mentioned the fact in parliamentary proceedings and it was duly recorded in *Hansard*.

The purpose of all depth charges is to damage a submarine so completely that it has to surface, whereupon it becomes vulnerable to attack from both sea and air. Conventional depth charges can be pretty useful but have to be accurately dropped to have the desired effect. The idea of a nuclear depth charge was that it would cause a much bigger sub-surface shock wave and thus be more effective over a wider area.

The day on which we were to fly the nuke was preceded by days of ground lectures on just about everything to do with nuclear weapons: how they worked, the effect they had, and the practices, rules and procedures one had to adopt in their use, including the requirement to turn two keys simultaneously to arm the beast. On the allotted day it was all something of an anticlimax in that we witnessed it being loaded to the aircraft with great ceremony, stayed glued to our checklists throughout the flight, flew it around a bit, landed back on deck and handed over to the next crew to do the same.

I have only seen a submarine carry out an emergency surfacing on one occasion. It was a Dutch boat that was participating in one of the NATO exercises in the North Atlantic and I happened to be flying nearby when he declared a major leak and came rapidly to the surface. Water cascaded off her sides as she settled back into the foaming patch of ocean and then limped back to port for repairs. My imagination ran riot around the idea of being on one of those things in an emergency like that or in a true wartime engagement.

In the late 1970s, at the height of my time as a rescue pilot on 771 Squadron at Culdrose, I had another submarine encounter. I was called into the CO's office and the door was closed behind me. This in itself was an odd departure from normal routine. It was explained to me that an American Boomer had signalled to say that she had a sailor on board with peritonitis, a dangerous and painful condition that usually results when the appendix goes beyond appendicitis and ruptures. Although the huge vessel had superb medical facilities alongside her racks of intercontinental ballistic missiles, a patient with peritonitis should really be handled in a fully equipped hospital ashore. The dilemma for the Boomer captain was that his strict orders were to never reveal his position when at sea. The US Department of Defense had given him dispensation to come to the surface for a maximum of five minutes somewhere to the south-west of England in order that his patient could be transferred ashore. It was made very clear to me that five minutes would be all the time we would have to spot the sub as she surfaced, make our way to her and carry out the stretcher lift. If we failed to achieve it in that time then the submarine was obliged to dive and resume her deep patrol (all part of the MAD philosophy designed to 'protect' the western world). When I asked whether the sailor would be recovered into the submarine if we failed to hit the deadline, all I received was a shrug.

I was given a sealed envelope with the sub's position in it and told not to open it until we were airborne. All I knew was that we would need a full tank of fuel and we would be going a long way. 'Smiler' Grinney was the diver I'd been flying with on and off for about a year by then but Leading Aircrewman Steve Branley was a relatively new recruit to the team. We'd been involved in his training and he was turning out to be a superb navigator. Doc Morgan was also a new face; he was going to look after the medical needs of our patient during the flight home. I opened our envelope, headed to the south-west and settled down for the hour's flight to reach the designated spot. Along the way we discussed whether it would be better to stay high and thus be able to see more of the surface of the ocean, or to trust our navigation and stay low in the knowledge that it would take us less time to descend to the submarine when she surfaced.

We never reached a conclusion and just split the difference in the hope that we'd get the best of both worlds.

We had timed it with plenty of room for error and so about half an hour after leaving the Scilly Isles we found ourselves flying wide orbits around a patch of relatively calm sea as we calculated and recalculated our navigation.

I was scanning the ocean ahead while the guys in the cabin had divided their angles of view into equal quadrants. Sure enough and bang on time I heard a cry from the cabin that the sea looked different in our three o'clock. At the same time I was called on the allocated radio frequency by a very American voice and the submarine began to appear. It's hard to find the proper adjective to describe the sudden emergence of a submarine as big as that... awesome, imposing, surreal? We could see that a door at the base of the conning tower, or 'sail' as submariners call it, was already opening. Two sailors were inching their way out of the door carrying a stretcher, just as I flared the Wessex to a 20-foot hover off to one side of the black monster. The decking was not just wet but also slimy along the narrow flat top of the hull where the missiles nestled.

As I slid sideways and over the forward part of the deck, Branley quickly lowered Smiler and Doc Morgan to the submarine, where they clipped themselves to the rope offered by the Yanks and unclipped themselves from the winch wire. The plan was that we would give them a few moments to converse with the Americans and assess the patient without us generating a howling gale over the top of them, but I was itching to go back in and reattach the winch wire as it was clear Smiler was having considerable difficulty keeping his footing on the wet black metal. After only a few moments we received the thumbs-up and moved back over the sub for the recovery. Picking up a diver with a stretcher was a relatively straightforward process we practised on a daily basis so we were able to get everybody back into the cabin quite slickly. By the time my team had strapped the stretcher securely to the floor of our aircraft and given me the go-ahead to climb away the submarine was all but lost to sight. The moment the sailors had re-entered the sail I had seen her blow her air tanks and she quickly and silently slipped beneath the surface. A sobering experience.

The submariner looked particularly relieved to be on his way to a hospital and the return flight to shore passed uneventfully. He waved at me and gave a firm thumbs-up as the team lifted him carefully into the waiting ambulance. We later learned that his operation had gone well, that he'd recovered after a couple of weeks and was eventually flown home to America. It felt good to have helped a submariner for once, instead of trying to destroy an entire crew.

CONDUCT UNBECOMING

THE WESSEX WAS A WONDERFUL airframe that served the Navy well for many years. At various stages in my naval career I flew three models: the Marks 1, 3 and 5. They were actually three quite different aircraft.

Let's get the Wessex 3 out of the way first, because it was the first one I flew, long before I made it into the Search and Rescue role. I hated the Wessex 3, truly loathed it, but that's not really fair to the aircraft, it's more about the circumstances in which I was flying it. I'd spent my first two operational years on the dear old *Ark Royal* flying Sea Kings. The flying was, for the most part, pretty dull but I had loved the ship, loved the places we travelled to and loved the people, the rites of passage I'd been through, and the sheer exhilaration of being on an operational aircraft carrier with big powerful jet aircraft launching day and night from a tiny metal runway. They say that the deck of an aircraft carrier is the most exciting place on earth. I don't think I'll ever disagree with that.

At the end of my time on board the *Ark* I received the standard notification of my next posting. Once you became a little more senior you could negotiate where you were going to go to next. As a very junior sub lieutenant you took what you were given.

I was given Portland. If you've never been to the little rocky island, joined by a small strip of shingle to the town of Weymouth in Dorset, you should go. You'll come away being really glad that you live somewhere else, anywhere, as long as it's not on Portland. They've closed it now, but back in the mid-1970s it was a busy naval harbour adjoined by an odd little airstrip that was only big enough to accommodate helicopters. I'm not one to moan but it was a big shock after the delights of Florida aboard a carrier. I'd flown home from Fort Lauderdale on day one of what turned out to be a fantastic run ashore for all the boys I'd left behind. A year and a half of flying from the *Ark* was summed up in my logbook by: 'Grayson has done well in his first front line squadron and, with experience, should make a good instructor.'

Portland was in fog when I arrived. Actually Portland was always in fog. Clear blue air would come all the way across the Atlantic, funnel its way up the English Channel, hit the cliffs of Portland and turn into fog. I joined the squadron, proposed to my girlfriend and put an offer on a little house. It wasn't long before some of these moves were revealed to me as being a touch premature.

I started my conversion to the Wessex 3. The job was to consist mainly of flying around the Channel participating in training exercises. We were to train the observers, a breed of navigator who were far more 'Navy' than the pilots would ever become. They usually took charge of the crew of the aircraft and, when we were the best-placed asset to see the whole picture, they would use all the ships within a 50-mile radius to coordinate pincer attacks on submarines their sonar operators had found and identified. The pilot's job was to simply take the observers where they wanted to go while they finely tuned their skills of command and control.

Most helicopters are broadly similar but you have to do a conversion course in order to learn about the airframe, the engines, the peculiar flight characteristics and so on. I entered into the spirit of the thing, not least because I was going to be flying a single-pilot aircraft rather than being part of a two-pilot team. The airframe was lovely but the engine felt a bit weird after the Sea King. I'd been used to having two very reliable Rolls Royce Gnome engines: press the start button and wait for them to smoothly accelerate up to a point where they were going fast enough to start the rotors turning. They did this using a big battery, very like a car's. But not the Wessex 3, oh no. The Wessex 3 you had to plug into a large trailer called a Houchin. The Houchin was towed towards your aircraft at breakneck speed by a member of the ground crew sitting astride a tractor. I don't mean something that looked like a tractor, it *was* a tractor. Granted, it was painted bright yellow, but it was your common-or-garden thirty-year-old tractor, no cab, just big old mudguards over the tyres.

The ground crewman would jump from the seat, start the diesel engine of his Houchin and then haul out a fat white tube not unlike the curly vent pipe you get on the side of a washing machine. He would plug this into an orifice in the side of the helicopter engine, give a cursory thumbs-up and then stand back against the wheel of his tractor with his arms folded, waiting to see you make a mess-up of starting the helicopter engine. By this time the Houchin had compressed a large reservoir of air which, when you wanted to start the helicopter, was exhausted down the white pipe and literally blew the engine up to a speed that might enable it to start. This happened in the space of about two seconds and, if you hadn't done the right things in the right order, there was an almighty whoosh followed by silence. At this point the ground crewman would saunter back to his Houchin with a definite smirk on his face. I hated starting the Wessex 3.

The conversion course was going OK and I was resigned to the eighteen months I would have to spend doing this job. I'd asked to go to Search and Rescue but nobody was yet listening. I moved on to the instrument-training part of the conversion. This is where you learn to rely on the cockpit dials to keep you upright and going in approximately the right direction when flying in cloud. It's a particularly nasty way to aviate in a helicopter. If you take your hands off the controls of an aeroplane it will want to continue flying forwards in a straight line. If you take your hands off the controls of a helicopter it wants to fall over on its back and kill you. Instrument flying is therefore a white-knuckle ride with your wide-open eyes constantly searching the instruments for signs of deviation while your hands try to wrestle the machine back on track.

In one very memorable flight my instructor decided to demonstrate how easy it was to become disorientated. (I hated him for it at the time, but it was to stand me in very good stead for years to come – both in my flying and in my subsequent career in entertainment simulation.) For instrument-flying practice the instructor looks out of the window while the student (me) wears a large white plastic structure off the end of his helmet to prevent him seeing anything other than the cockpit instruments. We climbed out over the English Channel with me sweating it out and the instructor dishing out increasingly difficult exercises to try. It was essential to fly smoothly and accurately or you'd soon be in trouble.

It was all going reasonably well and I was controlling a 30-degree banked turn to the right as we flew round and around in a circle. The instructor suddenly said, 'Close your eyes, keep them closed and hand the controls to me,' which I did. What he then did, without me knowing it, was very slowly and very smoothly to roll the aircraft upright and then into a 30-degree turn to the left. Now the brain is a very clever thing, but it can only arrive at conclusions from the information it gets. This information mainly comes from sight, sound, smell, taste, touch and balance. If you deny the sight information you've lost a big input and you tend to rely on the other senses much more heavily.

When you're in an aircraft you rely a good deal on balance. The fluid canals in your ear sense movement and your brain draws conclusions from that movement, but it can be fooled. I'd been flying round to the right for so long that the canals had gradually settled their fluids. Once the instructor took control, his roll to the left was so slow that my canals didn't sense the movement, so as far as I was concerned I was still in a right-hand turn. When he then performed a flick roll to the right through 60 degrees he was actually taking us back to the position I'd started from, but my brain said: You started at 30 degrees right, there's been a massive flick roll to the right, therefore you must be well on your way to being upside down. The instructor immediately told me to open my eyes, concentrate on my instruments and take back control.

Believe your instruments. Believe your instruments. Believe your instruments. We learn it over and over again but it's bloody hard to do when you brain is screaming, 'But you're upside down, you're upside down, we're all going to die.' I tried and I tried and I tried but I just couldn't shake off the certainty that we were upside down. We had to abandon the flight and return to Portland. No problem, we'd finish off the rest of the exercise in the next lesson – or so I thought.

At this point I must digress slightly to tell you about a small social problem that had emerged out of the woodwork. On the day I'd left the *Ark Royal* an old mate had asked if, once I got to Portland, I could order a bunch of tickets for the Portland Summer Ball. He would be back in time for the ball but not in time to qualify for any tickets. This wasn't a problem for me. I simply went to the wardroom on my first day at Portland, put down the names of the guests who would be coming (several of whom I'd never heard of) and put myself down as the host. My mate would then be paying me later.

A few days later I was called to the office of Wings. The captain is in full charge of all aspects of an airbase but Wings is in charge of all flying activities. As an aviator we feared Wings more than any other; he had total power over all pilots and we rarely even met the airbase captain. Nervously I knocked on Wings' door. 'Ah, come in, Grayson, sit down. Look, I don't know if you know what I'm talking about but one of the guests you've invited to the Portland Summer Ball is persona non grata here.' He went on to inform me that Lieutenant This and Lieutenant Commander That would be most welcome to attend, but I should not expect a ticket for Miss Such and Such.

It occurred to me to launch into a long explanation about how they weren't really my tickets and how I'd never heard of the lady in question. I decided instead that I'd simply accept the message and pass it on. It was no skin off my nose. After all, I wasn't even going to the ball. I responded, 'Yes, sir, certainly, sir, thank you, sir,' saluted smartly and hastily retreated from the lion's den.

Back to the flying, where my conversion training continued. Whoosh, bang, rumble: I was beginning to get the hang of starting the Wessex 3. Meanwhile, the story of the lady being barred from Portland had got out; not from me, it simply wasn't a significant enough thing for me to even bother mentioning. Some wag on another squadron (yes, I did learn who it was, but not until many years later) had a bit of a vendetta going with Wings and decided he could score heavily by anonymously complaining to the captain. The captain called Wings into his office, told him he couldn't just decide to exclude certain people from social events and sent him away with a flea in his ear. Wings, not surprisingly, concluded that I'd just dropped him right in it and from that moment my destiny was sealed.

I was preparing for my extra instrument-training flight – Nomex fireproof coverall, horrible sweaty goon suit, etc – when the squadron CO stuck his head around the corner. 'Don't bother getting dressed.

We've both got to go and see Wings, right now.' This was a peculiar turn of events but I was blissfully unaware of just how devastating the rest of the day was going to be. My CO went in first. He can't have been in there for more than a minute when he emerged from Wings' office and instructed me to follow him in.

'Stand there,' boomed Wings. 'Grayson, I understand you've been having problems with your instrument flying, that you've failed one of your conversion flights and that you're therefore going to need extra flights.' I was too flabbergasted to reply. He continued: 'Well, there's no place at Portland for less than fully operational pilots. I don't see any reason to continue wasting flying time on you. It will now be sent up to the Admiralty Review Board to decide what to do with you. That will be all.' My CO opened the door and we left.

By halfway through the afternoon I was on a train to somewhere else. I can't even remember where it was, I was in such a daze. I think it may have been Portsmouth. I'd learned during the long walk back to the squadron that the Admiralty Review Board was the two-day process by which the Navy dumped you out of the door. The CO had more or less apologised to me in a darkly mysterious way but he'd made it clear that there was absolutely nothing he could do about it.

Several months were to pass before I learned the full background story. Not only had Wings been embarrassed at being hauled up in front of the captain and told to rescind his 'persona non grata' decision, but the lady in question had been his mistress a couple of years earlier. Apparently she'd continued in that role right up to the day that Wings had dropped all his marbles off the table, driven to see her and given her a particularly nasty hiding. The Navy had put him in Netley mental hospital for a couple of years, rehabilitated him and then made him Wings at Portland. Good decision. Or so it must have seemed to him, right up until this snotty-nosed sub lieutenant had appeared out of nowhere and overturned his apple cart.

I was completely unaware of all this as I arrived at the Admiralty Review Board. All I knew was that my three years of hard work and training to do the job I'd always wanted to do was about to go firmly and squarely down the pan. Once again I thought about trying to give a long and involved explanation about ball tickets and flying upside down but it quickly occurred to me that they'd probably despatch *me* straight off to Netley. I decided to keep quiet, answer their questions openly and politely and see what came my way. Their lordships asked a lot of what they thought were deeply probing questions. They sent me for my standard half-hour with the psychiatrist who asked obscure questions about whether I'd had a pet dog and so on. Then they invited me back in to watch them grunting as they read through the piles of reports that quickly accumulate about you during a military career, however short that career had been. Finally they delivered their verdict. I would be given the opportunity of five hours' assessment flying with 'Standards Flight'. This was a small unit of very experienced pilots who were responsible for inspecting all the Fleet Air Arm squadrons and ensuring that the standard of naval aviation was kept high across the board. Once again I was in for a train ride, this time back to Culdrose in Cornwall, where all naval flying training is conducted.

My logbook records three trips with Standards Flight:

August 5th	50 minutes	General Flying Practice.
August 5th	55 minutes	Instrument Flying Practice.
August 6th	1 hour 40 minutes	Standards Check.

The last of these trips was with Lt Cdr Dave Mallock – something of an aviation god to a 21-year-old sub lieutenant. When we landed he asked me to go to the debriefing room and make him a cup of coffee. He came in, sat down, took a sip of his coffee, leaned forward and said, 'Jerry, I'm a bit confused. Why have you been sent here?'

I wanted to hug him. Finally here was someone who didn't approach the subject with any baggage. I unloaded my story all over him and he intermittently chuckled as I named the principal characters involved. One week later I was back on a front-line Sea King anti-submarine squadron. This time it was 814 Squadron on HMS *Hermes*. It wasn't the longed-for SAR and it wasn't the dear old *Ark* but at least I was still a naval aviator. I restarted plans for a wedding and was married just before Christmas 1976, then went off to sea for another six months.

Some years later I met Wings again for one last time. His position by then was Officer in Charge of the Royal Navy stand at the International Boat Show. (I was there to fly SAR demos over the pond just outside the National Exhibition Centre in Birmingham.) After watching him make something of an arse of himself in front of a large contingent of hard-bitten sailors I concluded that for once maybe justice had been done.

THE DISAPPEARING HUNTER

AFTER EIGHTEEN MONTHS SERVING OUT my time on the *Hermes* I finally made it to the job I really wanted: Search and Rescue. Each time the appointments officer came to *Hermes* to discuss the jobs that people would progress to next in their careers, he would scan down the list muttering, 'Let's see what we've got for you, Grayson,' at which point I would say with absolute confidence, 'I'm going to SAR on 771 Squadron, sir.' This would fluster him somewhat as it clearly wasn't what his list said at all. He was further unseated when the squadron CO confirmed that he'd understood all along that I would be going to SAR next. (I'd been telling him this with equal confidence for over a year.) Legend had it that some pilots languished for years in a single job. Whereas the normal tour was around two years, some name plaques seemed to drop off the appointer's wall planner and fall down the back of his radiator. Over time the appointer must have assumed that the error in my next appointment was his own and eventually he handed me the paper sending me to SAR. I was over the moon.

On SAR we took great pride in how quickly we could be airborne after hearing the scramble tones on the tannoy. It's still deeply ingrained in me. I once made an idiot of myself in Jersey airport when the flight announcement was preceded by exactly the same tones. I was up, out of the door and into the airport car park before I could stop myself.

In order to be able to make a quick getaway, our morning preparations had to be thorough. By the time the aircrew arrived in the morning, the ground crew had already been there for some hours, checking over the airframe, the engines and the various cockpit systems. They had often been there all night in order to change some life-expired parts or carry out items of unscheduled maintenance. If either the duty or the standby SAR aircraft needed more intensive maintenance, then the overnight engineering team would have swapped our equipment into one of the spare squadron aircraft. As we drove up to the squadron buildings in the dark and the cold of the early morning, we would usually find two aircraft sitting outside 'on the line' and the engineers preparing for a well-earned breakfast.

The crewman went out to prepare the rear aircraft cabin, check the standard on-board equipment package and lay out his personal navigation equipment in a preferred pattern. The diver, meanwhile, donned his bright orange wetsuit and double-checked all those particular items that divers attach to themselves. I'd take a look at the weather forecast, get the kettle on and, once everybody else had finished, go out to warm up each aircraft in turn. It was more a case of checking that they started at all. Despite the love and attention lavished on these aircraft they were still pretty old machines. Some of them had seen service in Aden and Korea – wars that had been fought before I was born.

For most of my time on SAR we used the Wessex 5, a wonderful aircraft with two Rolls Royce Gnome engines identical to the Sea King. However, when I first arrived we were still using the venerable Wessex 1 with only a single jet engine. It often seemed to me that the first thing a helicopter design team would decide upon would be the aircraft starting procedure. They must have constantly searched for new and amusing jokes in this department, which would then presumably keep everybody giggling throughout the rest of the design procedure. I've already described the whoosh of the Wessex 3. The Whirlwind 7, the forerunner of the Wessex and the helicopter on which I'd originally trained, was started by pulling a large ring under the 'dashboard'. This fired a twelve-bore shotgun cartridge – honestly, I'm serious – into the engine which would then set the twelve big pistons clattering away.

The Whirlwind 7 also had some anomalies when it came to stopping the big radial piston engine. You could get into a set of circumstances where the normal shutdown procedure didn't work at all. You then had to adopt a different procedure, which you'd usually forgotten. I found myself in this embarrassing position at five o'clock on a Friday afternoon during my initial training course. I'd been the last aircraft to land, the control tower had shut down the radio, and all my colleagues were streaming out of the squadron building and away on their weekend break. I was reduced to waving frantically from the cockpit to try to attract the attention of someone, anyone, who could remind me of how to stop the bloody thing. I had visions of still sitting there on Monday morning, waiting for the fuel to run dry.

The Wessex Mark 1 brought a new joke with it: the AVPIN starting system. It still used the shotgun cartridge (how the designers must have laughed at that one) but this time it initiated a controlled explosion in a particularly nasty fluid that didn't need oxygen to burn. The AVPIN fluid would burn almost instantaneously and the hot gases would shoot through a small starter turbine which would, in turn, start the engine. After suffering these explosions for some time the starter turbine would give up and, during the next start, spray a fine cocktail of AVPIN and molten metal shrapnel out of the side of the engine bay. The consequent machine-gun effect along the squadron windows would inevitably draw the attention of an amused crowd who would later give you marks for the style with which you exited your, by now, burning aircraft. The last part of the start-up checks consisted of: 'Open the cockpit door so you can run away if the engine blows up.' This would have been fine if the design team hadn't placed the pilot's seat on top of the engine. Your escape route therefore lay down the side of the engine. Good joke, guys! We really enjoyed it.

You can therefore see why there were always two aircraft kept ready on the line: the Duty and the Standby. If the Duty went up in flames while scrambling on a mission you went over to the Standby, leaving somebody else to put the fire out. I had to start both aircraft each morning before I could qualify for the diver's excellent fry-up of eggy-bakes. Once I'd shut each one down I would then leave all of the cockpit switches in exactly the right position for a quick restart and departure. It was tradition that, from that moment on, there was an exclusion zone around both the Duty and Standby SAR. If anybody wanted to enter, they came and asked the duty pilot for permission to do so. In this way you could be absolutely certain that you'd always find the aircraft exactly as you left it.

I would then retrace my steps into the squadron building and hang my bone dome on the hook provided for the purpose just inside the door. The bone dome is another unique form of torture inflicted on military aviators the world over. Anybody else would call it a flying helmet but, in the military, everything must have a nickname. The theory went that all aviators had to have bone where everybody else kept their brains, thus the protective covering must be the 'bone dome'. Once you'd worn in a bone dome it was a surprisingly comfortable fit. The leather interior moulded to your lumps and bumps and the earpieces fitted snugly around each ear. This enabled you to hear both the two exterior radios and the one internal intercom over the scream of a jet engine lying just beneath your feet. It also came with two visors: a clear one and a smoked one. Nobody ever used the clear visor because all it achieved was to distort your vision, but you carefully protected the useful smoked one from any scratches and polished it daily. The tiniest scratch in your peripheral vision could drive you insane while trying to hover accurately next to a cliff with the sun in your eyes. Nobody ever borrowed another pilot's bone dome; that was out of the question. It wouldn't fit you and, when you gave it back, it wouldn't fit the owner any more. We all dreaded the day when one or other of the earpieces burst. Not only would you have to spend the remainder of the flight with a warm trickle of glycerine oil down your neck but the sticky fluid would be absorbed by the leather and result in the need for a new bone dome. A week of agony would follow as the new bone dome moulded to your head.

With all the preparations complete, the three of us could settle down for a big breakfast and, if we were lucky, a read of the papers. It would usually be a long time before eight thirty when the rest of the squadron came to work so we had the place to ourselves. A TV in the corner of the crewroom was usually on, and I perfected the dual techniques of being able to fall instantly asleep and bring myself instantly one hundred per cent awake. I still have something of a reputation for it at late dinner parties.

On the morning of 6 July 1979 we were scrambled to an aircraft accident so bizarre that it made full-page coverage in all the national broadsheets and resulted in questions in Parliament. First the *dee-dah, dee-dah* of the scramble tones came over the tannoy. Anybody in the corridor would flatten themselves against the wall and anyone near a door would hold it open for you as you hurtled down the stairs and out of the door, grabbing the bone dome along the way. The thirty or so paces to the aircraft would be used in getting the bone dome on and firmly secured. The last couple of yards would see a change of step that allowed a perfect launch up the side of the big helicopter: right foot on the wheel, left foot in the stirrup, right foot in the next stirrup and left foot in through the cockpit door. Get it the wrong way round and you had tied yourself in knots before even reaching the cockpit.

The diver was rarely more than two paces behind you while the crewman stayed behind for ten seconds to write down the details of the job. We usually stayed 'crewed-up' as a team for several months in order to get used to each other's little foibles and to be able to communicate without speaking. In theory anybody could replace anybody else. In practice you came to rely very heavily on your crew and often owed your lives to each other from some previous excursion. Detlef Wodak was still with me as the crewman and we had the most experienced diver in the Navy with us in the form of Scotsman Jamie Bauld. We all called him Granddad but he was probably under forty, maybe even younger.

I'd heard 'Hunter ejection in the Bristol Channel' as I flew out of the door. It took us about 90 seconds to flash up and launch, by which time we knew that an RAF pilot twenty miles out over the Bristol Channel had been forced to 'bang out' of his stricken aircraft – cause unknown. As we raced towards the north coast the story unfolded over the radio. First we heard that he'd given a good position report in his Mayday call, then that a parachute had been sighted. The RAF controller at St Mawgan was talking both to us and to an RAF Search and Rescue helicopter that had launched from Chivenor at exactly the same time. As the splash-down point was nearly equidistant from our two airbases it became clear that we were each going to arrive at exactly the same time. If anything I had a tiny head start.

The other helicopter called 'Ten miles to run' and I answered with 'Rescue Two One has nine miles'. If we weren't very careful we were going to run into each other at a combined closing speed of over 200 mph. However, more dangerous than this was the prospect of it becoming known that a Navy rescue team had saved an RAF jet pilot. I knew this wasn't going to be allowed to happen and, sure enough, the RAF controller tasked the RAF helicopter to go to the RAF parachutist while we were freshly tasked with going to reports of an unidentified incident in the village of Tintagel.

On our way there we could hear that the RAF pilot had been successfully plucked from the sea and was on his way to the hospital in Plymouth with back injuries. In the meantime the radio was revealing more details of the incident in Tintagel: it involved the rescued pilot's aircraft, which had turned around, flown back inland and crashed.

As any student of mythology knows, Tintagel is the site of King Arthur's famous castle. Lady Guinevere, Merlin the magician and brave Sir Lancelot are reputed to have spent their summers in the magnificent clifftop setting. The outline of the walls are still there. Getting to the castle involves a precarious climb down slippery rocks and up the other side to a promontory that's almost an island. It's worth the effort – a truly magical place at any time of the year as you look down over 200 feet to the sea below. Back from the cliff edge there lies about a half mile of flat, small and unkempt fields, each defined by a drystone Cornish wall. Then you arrive at the village of Tintagel, a not-very-pretty village strung out along the road that runs parallel to the coast. Most of the houses are semi-detached and decorated in pebbledash. There aren't many of them and you wonder how anybody scrapes a living in such a place. If it wasn't for the annual influx of summer visitors they probably wouldn't be able to.

We half expected to see a black plume of smoke rising from the area as we approached it but nothing was obvious. The radio had gone quiet as the emergency services anxiously awaited our first report. The village seemed fine, nothing out of the ordinary there, so we carried on down to the castle and scanned the cliffs for sign of the wreckage. Still nothing. I called the controller at St Mawgan to ask if he was sure it was Tintagel that had suffered the impact as many of the Cornish villages have very similar names and most of them begin with a 'T'. He assured me that phone calls were still coming in from residents in the village and that police, fire and ambulance were all on their way. Jamie Bauld was talking to the local coastguard station on his separate VHF radio and they had assured him that the Hunter jet had indeed come down in the village and that they also had teams on their way.

We headed back towards the village knowing that we had the best possible vantage point from which to home in on the epicentre of the problem – we just couldn't find it. We were beginning to get that fear that runs down the neck when you suspect you might have done something really silly. Suddenly Jamie shouted, 'Turn round, boss, turn around.' The Wessex came sharply round to the right but as I looked down the side of the helicopter I still couldn't see what he was gesticulating at. He'd spotted a hole in a wall and beyond it another and beyond that yet another. I took the helicopter down very low and we lined up the holes in the wall by sight. Sure enough there was a light furrow dug across the fields and passing through each successive drystone wall. It could have been made by an aircraft that still hadn't fully settled to the ground but, if so, where the hell had the aircraft gone?

We followed the furrow back to the village but there were no signs of aircraft debris along the way and, as we climbed over the village, it was clear that the furrow didn't continue across the road and into the fields beyond, as one might have expected. It began to cross my mind that the pilotless aircraft might have taken off again, but gone where? As I turned back around for another look at this peculiar trail, Detlef spotted it. 'There, there.' He pointed from the open cabin door. Jamie and I followed the line of his pointing finger but could only make out two undamaged houses separated by a walkway between them, just wide enough for two wheelbarrows to pass. In the walkway was what appeared to be a ladder and a few bits of old timber propped against the side of one of the houses. As we circled once more I suddenly realised what we were looking at. Far from being a few bits of timber, we were looking along the wing of the jet, perfectly balanced on its side and wedged into a position that you couldn't have got it into with a crane, however hard you tried.

This is the *Daily Telegraph* report of the event:

At the home of Mr Theodore Wilson, 67, a retired bank manager, his decorator Mr Ivan Irons, was working up a ladder at the back of the house. 'I heard this colossal noise and my first thought was that the American Space Laboratory Skylab had come crashing to earth. I just had time to slip down the ladder and get a few yards away before something smashed my ladder to smithereens.

'If the pilot had tried a thousand times he could never have wedged his aircraft between those two buildings like this one did, and this one didn't have a pilot!'

Wreckage of the plane landed within ten yards of a garage where a tanker carrying 1,500 gallons of petrol was preparing to unload. The driver, who had been 'taking cover', leapt into his cab and drove the tanker to a nearby field. Witnesses later praised his quick thinking act of courage.

We landed in a field across the road from this strange scene and Jamie nipped through the hedge to find the bodies. But there weren't any. There was a rather flat car in the garage, one man had hurt his back running away from the accident and a lady who had been hanging her washing in the garden (when the jet had landed

and taken the washing line out of her hands) was being treated by an ambulance man for shock. As Jamie was nearly run over crossing the road it became clear that, unusually, we'd been about the last to reach the scene.

We were too low to call St Mawgan and fill them in on the situation so we took off, climbed to a thousand feet and filed our report. We were immediately tasked to run off to the RAF base and pick up a senior officer to come and take charge of their abandoned machinery. This probably wasn't quite what he'd had in mind when he came to work that morning and he looked oddly out of place with his moustache and smart cap as we deposited him back in the centre of Tintagel. We hung around for a few minutes longer just to make sure there was nothing else we could help him with but there was only one small task he wanted us to perform once he'd assessed the situation. Would we mind, he asked, climbing back to a height from where we could talk to his base and informing them of two things: first, that there were live ammunition rounds on board the aircraft and he would need a team of armourers to render them safe. And, second, that he'd forgotten to bring any money with him, so could he have the base commander's authorisation to make a reverse-charge telephone call back to the base? Ours is not to question why, so we took off once more in our £2,000 per hour machine and duly filed his request for a ten-penny phone call.

We headed home. If we were lucky we'd be back in time for lunch.

A few days later, following a question in Parliament about continued low flying in the area, an aircraft exclusion zone was instigated around the village, which lasted for several years. The inhabitants had had a lucky escape.

GRAND PRIX

I HAD KNOWN FROM AN EARLY AGE that I wanted to be a pilot but my other big love in life has always been motor racing. My father was a car mechanic by trade but he'd worked his way up the ladder and, by the time I was about seven or eight years old, had become sales director of our local Ford dealership in Chichester. Every year the big boys of Formula One would make their annual pilgrimage to Goodwood, the two and a half miles of tarmac racetrack that lay a couple of miles away from home. It was the early days of Lotus, Colin Chapman, and the fabulous British partnership between Jim Clark and Graham Hill. The pits at Goodwood were very basic, no more than a wooden counter protected by a corrugated iron roof; the accurate restoration by Lord March means they can still be seen today. Lord March has even put up the old advertising hoardings and at the annual revival meeting in September each year they still play the musical marketing slogans from the time of my childhood over the loudspeakers. It's a weird experience for me.

The lack of track facilities meant that the teams had to find a local garage from which to base themselves and, as luck would have it, Lotus came to my father's emporium at Rowes of Chichester. I was woken early one Sunday morning and couldn't believe my eyes when we reached the workshop. It was bursting at the seams with racing cars from the support events: Huge V8 Ford Galaxies and Falcons bigger than any car I'd ever seen, with long fins extending down each rear wing. The big treat lay in the paint shop which had been especially cleaned and tidied to accommodate the two gleaming Formula One cars in traditional British Racing Green with a stylish yellow line down the side. I thought I was in heaven when the chief mechanic lifted me into the seat that Jim Clark would be sitting in later that day.

The family connection with Goodwood went on for many years. The old wartime airfield ceased to be an active racetrack in the mid-1960s but reopened later as a flying school. My father used a little spare money left to him by my grandfather and became the first student to get his Private Pilot's Licence there; I was very proud. Some years later I would reverse the trend and, as a professional pilot, use the money left to me by my father to learn to motor-race. At the end of the 1960s we moved away from Chichester; I completed my O Levels and went on to study for A Levels with a view to becoming an airline pilot. Suddenly and without any warning British Airways (BOAC as it was then) shut down their airline pilot school at Hamble. The independent airline British Eagle had gone to the wall and left many pilots available for hire; there was no longer any need to fund a training school. I was devastated, and began to take less and less interest in my A Levels. I stopped taking Physics because I didn't remotely understand it and since I'd only been studying Maths in order to support the Physics I stopped doing that as well. That left me with Geography, a subject I loved but which would hardly keep me fully occupied by itself.

Halfway through the A Level course we were interviewed by the careers master, a wonderful old pipe-smoker from an army background. 'What the bloody hell's the matter with you, man?' he asked with a typical lack of ceremony. He brushed aside my moaning about the closure of the Hamble Flying School with: 'Well, you'd better join one of the armed services, they've got aeroplanes coming out their ears.' From the armful of military recruiting brochures he handed me there was only one picture that really caught my eye: that of a naval helicopter pilot. He seemed to be having a whale of a time and so, just a few weeks later, I was going through the pilot aptitude tests at the joint services assessment centre at Biggin Hill. In the days that followed I went for my officer selection course and, at the end of the three-day exercise, I was called in before their lordships. I'd passed all the tests and had a reasonable aptitude for flying but they would prefer it if I stayed at school and gained my A Levels first. I was, after all, only just approaching my seventeenth birthday.

With the bravado of youth I haughtily announced that this wasn't an option. I was going to drop out of A Levels at the halfway mark and they either took me straight away or I was off to one of the other services. I cringe now to even think of being so cavalier with an offer like that. It threw them a bit, but about a week later an envelope turned up in the post suggesting that, as the minimum joining age was seventeen and a half, they didn't feel they could take me on right away but they were prepared to offer me a flying scholarship. This was a system by which the Navy funded sixth-formers to take a civilian PPL course, after which they could be considered for a military career. I leapt at the chance and by the beginning of August I was back at Goodwood, serving drinks in the jockeys' bar by night and flying aircraft all day. If I thought I'd died and gone to heaven the effect was compounded on the day the March Formula One team adopted Goodwood as their practice circuit and it became apparent that they had set aside the month of August for their new driver to learn the new car. His name was Niki Lauda.

In the classroom we learned the finer points of meteorology, the theory of flight, navigation, radio procedures and a dozen other subjects. Then we'd get airborne and put them into practice. Although I was aiming at being a helicopter pilot, everybody first learned on fixed-wing aeroplanes. It wasn't a highly pressurised course. If I was ever missing from the ground school, they'd send someone over to the pit wall where I could inevitably be found sitting chatting to Mr Lauda, his mechanics and Mick the Goodwood Fireman. It was bliss – and the sun shone for the whole month too.

Goodwood has drawn me back at various stages in my career. When I later became a film pilot I based my helicopter there for the filming of the James Bond movie *A View to a Kill*, and it was dear old Mick who refuelled me every day. But the Grand Prix circus had moved to new pastures and it was to Silverstone and Brands Hatch that I would pilgrimage each year, never missing the British Grand Prix until I joined the SAR.

I could usually swap my place on the duty roster to ensure that the mid-July weekend was kept free until, in 1979, there was nobody to swap with. Everybody had prior commitments and I had exhausted every possibility. The squadron CO walked into the morning briefing and was crestfallen to announce that he'd been 'volunteered' to take charge of the Air Day raffle ticket sales effort. The raffle habitually raised many thousands of pounds towards worthy naval charities but its revenue had been waning and the CO was charged with improving results. He wanted us all to think long and hard about events taking place before the August Air Day at which there would be plenty of people to whom we could sell raffle tickets. I didn't have to think too hard and shot up my hand.

'The British Grand Prix, sir. There's a hundred and twenty thousand people there. They've all got money in their pockets.

We could put on an air display and provide an air ambulance service in exchange for being allowed to send Wrens out among the crowd selling raffle tickets in uniform.'

The whole squadron laughed out loud. I think the CO had local village fetes in mind, but he was prepared to let me give it a go. Finally a door of opportunity had opened.

I'd been racing single seat Formula Fords at Silverstone for about a year so I had all the right names and numbers to contact but I wasn't too sure I could pull it off. Then I read in that week's *Autosport* that the British Racing Drivers' Club were to hold a special opening of their new medical facilities at the track. The opening would be on the first day of Grand Prix weekend. I got straight on the phone to George Smith, the track director. He was a jolly man with a great sense of humour but his bark could also be severe. It was a mammoth event to organise each year and he didn't take prisoners along the way. I put the suggestion to him and held my breath.

'You wanna do what? Are you seriously suggesting that you're going to give me a helicopter ambulance for the weekend and all I've got to do is let a few birds in suspenders sell raffle tickets? You're on. Give Sid Watkins a ring [the medical professor in charge of all Formula One affairs, always known as Prof] and sort out the details.'

'Actually,' I pressed, 'we usually like to have a second aircraft available in case we have problems with the first.'

He didn't think there'd be room to park two but he'd take both if we could squeeze them in. I was ecstatic. Not only was I off to the Grand Prix after all but I was going to be a *part* of it. I started ringing around and planning.

The British Grand Prix is the largest gathering of helicopters in the UK and, for one day a year, it counts as the busiest airport in the world. Silverstone, like Goodwood, is a converted wartime airfield and they didn't get around to improving the access by road until the year 2000, so all the teams, the drivers, the mechanics, the sponsors and every guest with the slightest claim to importance habitually travel by helicopter. Over 4,000 landings are made during the day as around 150 helicopters vie for the same small piece of aerial real estate. I still believe it's the greatest test of airmanship that any rotary pilot ever undertakes. My planning for our flights had to be meticulous. Plus there was the medical side of it to worry about, what equipment we'd need on board, where the local hospitals were situated and the procedures to follow in the event of a major accident. I detailed off the engineering department to worry about providing the Wrens for the raffle ticket sales and set about designing an air display to entertain the crowds all round the track during the lunchtime break. The Red Arrows were also due to perform, so our timings had to be accurate.

Departure morning arrived and it seemed that every man and his dog had found some essential reason for being a part of the crew. Both Wessex were topped to the gunwales with people, equipment and raffle tickets. They were so heavy we were going to have to stop at the Royal Naval Air Station at Yeovilton and then again at RAF Brize Norton just to have enough fuel to get there. The CO would be flying the second aircraft. I was a bit surprised when he walked into the flight briefing and announced that he would lead the trip. I hadn't had time to brief him at all, he had no idea of the scale of the bun-fight we were about to join in with, but he was adamant that this would be how we'd play it and he was, after all, the CO.

We refuelled twice without problems and set off towards the county of Northampton. Even having been there many times on the ground I was impressed to see Silverstone from the air. The distinctive ribbon of tarmac was surrounded by many new grandstands erected for the event and every available square inch of the infield was crammed with trucks and tents and hospitality areas, racing cars, people, and more racing cars. There wasn't much time to enjoy the view as I followed behind the CO's aircraft, checking all the time that he was picking up the arrival landmarks I'd hastily scribbled on a scrap of paper for him. The tarmac fixed-wing runway was obvious and, beside it, the grass area for the helicopters. We called 'finals' on the radio and made our approach to the grass. We were destined for an area close to the racing pits where the shiny new medical facility had been built. I could see it in the distance, defined by ropes and a large 'H', but between where we were now hovering and our destination lay the Formula Three paddock.

The paddock is the area where the racing cars are made ready and where all the real work is done as mechanics toil through the night to repair their cars from the previous race and prepare them for the next. This often involves stripping engines and gearboxes down to their smallest components, cleaning them, inspecting them and reassembling them. They did it so often that it must have been second nature to them but it involved covering long work benches in white tablecloths and laying everything out in a very precise order. I watched in horror as the CO ahead of me took the first big Wessex and its associated wind storm in a straight line towards the medical centre via the Formula Three paddock. He was certainly high enough to be safe and, in normal circumstances, it wouldn't have done any damage, but a tablecloth can travel quite a long way if you give it enough impetus and at least half a dozen of them took flight as I watched. It was strange how they seemed to accelerate away from the paddock. In retrospect they were probably becoming lighter as they shed themselves of the various nuts, bolts, washers and springs that comprise a modern racing gearbox.

I found the other route towards the medical centre and settled on to the grass behind the first Wessex, but I was in no hurry to shut down the engines and rotors as the CO seemed to be engaged in meaningful discussion with a large crowd of mechanics who were still streaming through the rope barrier. In due course they moved off as a pack towards the administration offices and by the time I'd secured my own aircraft the CO was by himself. At this exact point a runner arrived and politely requested that we called in on Mr George Smith. We left the rest of the party to unload and threaded our way towards George's office via a sea of racing folk who all spared a brief second in their otherwise frenetic weekend to pause and point. I was mortified but could only dejectedly lead the boss towards where I knew our destiny lay.

Sure enough George was waiting at his desk. I'd have taken it better if he'd gone berserk but he just looked so sad and kept shaking his head. He'd just suffered an onslaught from every team manager in the Formula Three fraternity, he didn't really know what to say and I felt we'd badly let him down. We mooched back to our landing pad and agreed on how we'd get in and out of there in future while, as we later found out, the Formula Three managers chartered a small jet to fly to Germany and bring back a rather large number of replacement gearboxes.

Thankfully it was all forgiven and forgotten by the next morning and we went on to have a successful weekend. We performed in the display, our ambulance services weren't required and the Wrens sold all their raffle tickets. I thought it couldn't get any better but there was one more surprise for me on Grand Prix day itself. An hour before the start of the main race, one of my friends from the racing driver school came hurtling over in a pick-up truck and indicated that I should jump in the back. We bumped our way over to the school as he explained that each Grand Prix car was to be lead around the track to the grid by a school car with the Formula One driver's national flag flying from the roll bar. One of the boys had failed to turn up and they needed me to drive – the gods were shining on me again. With great excitement I leapt into the racing car, threw on a helmet and could just make out the public broadcast system announcing that the

Brazilian driver Carlos Pace was being led by the pilot of the rescue helicopter. It was a moment to savour.

The postscript to Silverstone 1979 came in November when I dressed up in naval black tie for the annual Jim Russell Racing School dinner and dance. A parade of young tigers went up to receive their prizes, including one who would later go on to win the Indianapolis 500. Derek Bell was presenting the prizes, a driver who has almost lost count of the number of times he's won at Le Mans and a man who was definitely high on my list of heroes. Completely out of the blue they announced: 'The most promising new driver of the year', followed by my name. I rose in a daze amidst the applause and made my way to the platform when suddenly George Smith stood up, pointed in horror and shouted, 'Aaaaaah, it's him!' I bought him his beer for the rest of the night.

But this was not to be the end of the story. The following year the Grand Prix alternated back to Brands Hatch and we were invited to repeat our role. This time we just took one aircraft and I parked it right in the middle of the circuit, just behind the pits. I'd taken a skeleton rescue crew and didn't have to worry about selling raffle tickets, we could simply sit on the grass for three days and enjoy the racing. We had to move our helicopter sideways on the second day to make room for an RAF Harrier jump jet, who amused us enormously by doing far more damage to the Formula One paddock than we could even have attempted the year before. The circuit management sent over a crate of beer for us and we spent the night before the race with the Lotus mechanics as they toiled under sodium lights to prepare Mario Andretti's car for the main event.

The following morning we had some work to do. Halfway through a race for historic cars, many of them without seat belts, one of the drivers lost his machine in a big way going through Clearways corner right in front of us and did an awful lot of damage to himself.

We manned up, flashed up and were soon on our way to the hospital at Woolwich. By the time we returned to Brands Hatch, 'Prof' Watkins had heard from the surgeons that they'd found massive internal bleeding and had only been able to save the driver as a result of how quickly he'd been delivered to them. If he'd gone by road he'd be history himself. From that day forwards the Navy always provided the ambulance at the British Grand Prix while all the other Formula One venues around the world were requested to provide a helicopter. I beamed with pride some years later while sitting at home watching the television. The start of the French Grand Prix was delayed for twenty minutes as a direct result of the air ambulance being absent from its place of duty. Prof Watkins had decreed that never again should a Grand Prix be started unless a helicopter was ready and in place. Maybe we do all get a chance to make one small difference in this life.

'WHERE ARE WE GOING?'

IT IS THE CULTURE AMONG AVIATORS to always admit their mistakes. Within both civilian and military flying organisations are several systems by which you can make these admissions anonymously, without fear of recrimination. The net result is that everybody benefits from everybody else's mistakes and, hopefully, many accidents and incidents are thus avoided. When you put this together with the naturally self-deprecating humour of a navy man you could easily end up concluding that most of us are inadequate buffoons who should never be allowed near a flying machine. I prefer to think that the culture of telling the lurid details of one's screw-ups is a healthy and positive thing to embrace.

Any aviator, whether amateur or professional, will probably have a dozen or so stories to tell of getting lost. It can end tragically, as weather or night closes in and the aviator gradually and then totally runs out of options. We've all fallen into the trap at some time or another but thankfully most of us escape with nothing more than dented pride and an experience to draw on in the future.

Planning has always been the foremost discipline learned at the start of a career in aviation. With good planning you are much less likely to fall into the trap of diminishing options, and the more you reduce the normal cockpit workload the more spare capacity you have to deal with the unexpected. To this day I get laughed at by my family for reading the operator's manual from cover to cover before beginning to operate any new piece of equipment, whether it's a vehicle, a microwave oven or an iPod. Planning a flight is an essential part of the process, even if only to be sure that you have sufficient fuel on board to complete the task, or to be sure that you aren't about to cause chaos by wandering into some form of restricted, controlled or prohibited airspace. I also learned very early on to commit all the pieces of the planning puzzle to memory. Like in a car, the airflow in a helicopter usually flows from the rear to the front of the cabin, as I found to my cost the day my map was sucked from my grasp through the open window, along with my fuel calculations, notes on necessary radio frequencies and everything else I needed for the flight.

Since that day, despite a generally appalling memory, I've always seared the planning into my head and I think it stood me in particularly good stead during rescue operations. Questions like: 'How long can I stay here before I need to go for fuel?' or 'As soon as this casualty is on board what is the quickest way to the hospital?' are best asked in advance of the critical moments and not at the time when your brain capacity is already overloaded. A few minutes saved here and there by good mental planning could save someone's life.

On the other hand, we all get tired, we all get sloppy and we all get lazy at some point. It's often said about flying that it's 99 per cent boredom and 1 per cent pure terror, but the boring patches can be the ones that jump up and bite you. Let me return to Sea Kings for a short story about boredom…

A Sea King crew in the anti-submarine role was comprised of two pilots, an observer and a sonar operator. Both active and passive sonar would be used. Active sonar 'pings' a sound into the ocean while the operator waits to hear a return echo that indicates something is there; with passive sonar the operator listens for the sound of a submarine's engine or propeller wash. A really good sonar operator can determine the name of a submarine from the sound made by the screws (propellers), as each one has slightly different characteristics.

The sonar operator is therefore an extremely alert crewmember for all four hours of an anti-submarine sortie. The observer is similarly attentive to detail as he plots all other air, surface and sub-surface activity on his radar. But for a pilot, at night, in a two-man cockpit crew, it can be monotonous. We used to swap controls every thirty minutes and while the flying pilot maintained his night vision by looking outside, the non-flying pilot was responsible for monitoring the instrumentation. Staring at a set of illuminated dials, none of which is actually moving, can be mind-numbing, so we would set ourselves other little tasks, like peeling an orange in such a way as to be an utterly pith-free work of art at the end of thirty minutes.

When using active sonar we would often be hovering over the ocean for up to an hour at a time while the body of the sonar transducer dangled into the sea, held by a piece of electrical wire from beneath the helicopter. To keep the wire vertical the Sea King had to be operated in an autopilot setting, so the pilot with his hands on the controls wasn't really flying it at all, just monitoring the systems. The only excitement would be transiting to an alternative but equally anonymous point over a deserted ocean. Passive sonar operations raised the boredom stakes to new intensities. Instead of hovering over the ocean with just the faintest chance of seeing a shark or a flying fish, you were confined to five hours (note that a helicopter uses less fuel in the cruise than in the hover) of droning around at 5,000 feet while the sonar operator listened to weak radio signals from little sonar buoys that had been parachuted from our helicopter to the surface of the sea.

Some time after I'd left the anti-submarine world the pilots developed a new game. It started innocently enough when one of the gauges on the instrument panel had failed and a pilot had enterprisingly used his pocket knife to prise the offending gauge from its socket, fix it and replace it. His co-pilot took a photograph of him doing it, which so excited everybody else that the competition began to see who could dismantle the most number of instruments, take a picture, then replace them all before landing. Once the squadron commander caught wind of the competition, of course, it had to stop. But by that time it had pretty much been won by the crew who had quietly circulated a photograph of themselves at 5,000 feet with every single instrument in the cockpit hanging out by its wires, and both pilots stark naked.

But I've digressed from the thread of the story I was trying to tell, in this case about getting lost. It was important to us that the Search and Rescue squadron maintained a good relationship with the local community. Helicopters can be a noisy and irritating intrusion when you're holding a wedding party on the lawn or just trying to grab a weekend siesta, so we did all we could to educate the local populace about who we were, what we did and how we did it. Sometimes this would simply consist of an evening slide show presentation to the local chapter of the Women's Institute culminating in the noisy inflation of a life raft, but more often than not we would be asked to provide a helicopter display at an annual fete. Displays involved a lot of planning and a mountain of paperwork. The other problem was that a local village fete never happened in a wide open space big enough for us to perform; even the simplest of displays would need something bigger than a football pitch in order to avoid sending the neat rows of trestle tables flying into the next village. Thus it was that the 'Guess the Height' competition was born. This avoided the need to come to a hover, gave us the chance to send along information pamphlets, and gave the squadron CO the opportunity to say yes to requests without fear of complications.

The Guess the Height stall was a great success at most local events, took a few pennies for the local charity and simply involved our aircrew flying once over the event and then phoning in the height at which the pass had been conducted. It was about the easiest thing you could ever be asked to do. On the day in question we had been denied any rescue call-outs and so there was a definite lack of adrenalin coursing through the veins as we ambled out for a sedate start-up procedure and headed off in the general direction of Falmouth, a large and historic Cornish port. Nice sunny day, temperatures and pressures all good, helicopter flying smoothly…

'Where are we going?' I casually asked Shep Woolley, my laconic and much-trusted crewman.

'Oh ha ha ha!'

'What do you mean, *ha ha ha*? *Where* are we going?'

'No, no, no, don't do this to me, boss.'

'Don't do *what* to you? I just want to know where the fete is. It's not a complicated question.

'I thought you knew, boss. I have no idea where we're going.'

'But you're the bloody navigator. You always navigate. How am I supposed to know where we're going?'

And so it went on, mainly in jest but with an undercurrent of awareness that we had both behaved too casually and entirely unprofessionally. The situation descended into farce as no amount of memory-wracking brought the answer any closer and even a radio call to our coastguard officer failed to throw light on the issue. Meanwhile, we'd crossed over Falmouth and couldn't think of anything to do beyond returning to base and trying to track down the

CO at home to ask exactly what it was he'd committed us to doing. We retraced our steps, rather chastened by our foolishness. As I returned to the crewroom I walked past a ringing phone, picked it up and was astonished to hear the fete organiser thanking me profusely for our attendance right over the top of her event and particularly thanking us for making two passes. Job done, time for a cup of tea.

Another of our PR efforts was to give a small display at local events, and one of these was the Hayle Lifeboat Fete. Hayle lies on the north Cornish coast, just to the east of St Ives, a promontory famous for its natural light, which has drawn painters for centuries. Hayle is separated from the sea by a magnificent white beach stretching for over three miles, but the town itself is a working fishing village and therefore often has cause to be thankful to the lifeboat service. On 25 August 1980, the day of the fete and the height of the school summer holidays, we were flat out. By the end of the day we had flown eight sorties and set a new record for six call-outs in one day.

The usual routine was to start at dawn and hand over to the afternoon crew at midday, or start at midday and stay on duty until darkness. We liked to be dressed and ready to go in good time, or even a bit earlier than the formal handover time (known in the Navy as 'warming the bell'), so when a call came in at 11.43 it was sensible for us to take it instead of the off-going crew, who might otherwise be airborne for hours.

My crew for the day was the crew with whom I operated for much of 1980 right up until my last flight in the Navy. The winchman was the ever dependable and wry-humoured Shep Wooley. I probably knew his real name at the time but to us he was always Shep. Our diver was Scouse Slater, whose real name was Lawrence, but more of that later. They were each occasionally replaced for a flight or two by someone else and complications were avoided on days when Scouse Hogan (who went on to become an extremely senior officer in Australian naval intelligence) replaced Scouse Slater. Scouse is of course the universal slang name for a Liverpudlian but rarely have I heard one as broad as Scouse Slater.

First out of the box was a call to an injured 23-year-old man who had fallen down a cliff. The number of people who manage to injure themselves this way each year would make your hair curl. From our airborne vantage point it was always blindingly obvious to us that erosion occurs just beneath the crust of a cliff in such a way that the last couple of feet will never support the weight of a man, but the tourist visitors to Cornwall and indeed many of the locals seemed unaware of this simple fact. If there was only one message I could convey in all these stories it would be this: *Never ever go anywhere near the edge of a cliff – it will kill you.*

When going to a 'shout' at which we knew there was a casualty who would benefit from medical attention before being lifted, we would take a doctor. In this case it was Steve Ormerod. We arrived at the scene; the coastguard on site set off a smoke flare to alert us to the position and also to give us an accurate local wind direction. We lowered Steve, who then asked for Scouse to bring down a stretcher. The casualty was about 150 feet down the cliff face at Gwennap Head with head injuries and a broken wrist. The pick-up went smoothly and we left Mr Findlay, a tourist from Kent, in the care of the medics at Treliske Hospital. Strike One.

Next up came a call-out from the coastguard to go to Kennack Sands, only five miles south of our base at Culdrose. It had been reported that a boy and a girl were in trouble in the water. We scrambled at 14.13, were airborne by 14.15 and 'on scene' at 14.19. Just as we started our search the coastguard called us to say that the missing kids had already been rescued by people from the beach and had been taken away by car. A successful completion and we never minded how it was achieved as long as people were kept alive and well. Strike Two.

By this time the Hayle Lifeboat Fete was in full swing. We'd already let the lifeboat know that we would be a bit late and he'd held off his display until we could get there. We had long ago worked up a show with the lifeboat at locations where a public address system could generate a little rescue story and keep the crowd informed of what was going on. First someone would jump into the water from the quayside and be designated as the 'casualty'. He would inflate his lifejacket and set off a flare. Around the corner of the quay would come the big orange lifeboat at full speed, demonstrate his manoeuvrability in the small harbour and then successfully recover the casualty. Then the announcer would declare that the casualty had been assessed by the lifeboat crew as being in need of medical attention and so a helicopter had been summoned. We would make our own appearance at high speed and low level. Cue more smoke which would swirl dramatically as I stood the big old Wessex on to her tail in order to stop directly over the lifeboat. Down would go the diver with a stretcher, the casualty would be hoisted aboard, and off we'd go at high speed to the rapturous applause of the audience. Such was the known and practised routine as we approached Hayle.

But the lifeboat threw us a curve ball by suggesting that we pick up the survivor from the water as he'd just jumped in from the quayside and wasn't wearing a lifejacket. No problem, down into the hover and crewman Shep lowered Scouse straight into the water right next to the casualty… at which point the casualty punched Scouse. Shep was incredulous and kept up the usual running commentary but instead of 'Left two, down three' it was more like the radio broadcast from a boxing match: 'He's trying to rip off Scouse's mask, Scouse has got him round the throat, oh no, he's broken free, Scouse has decked him one, he's trying to get the strop around the survivor's waist…' and so on. Eventually the Liverpudlian's strength and stamina paid off and the pair of them were on their way up the winch, courtesy of Shep. He left me with: 'Hang on, boss, I'm going to unplug and sort this out.' I could never see what was happening in the cabin beneath me, I had to rely entirely on whatever Shep was telling me, so the action of unplugging left me blind for a few seconds. When he plugged back in Shep was laughing as he told me that the moment the guy had been hauled into the cabin he'd punched Scouse again and tried to throw himself out of the cabin door. Shep had promptly returned the favour and the pair of them now had the guy securely fastened back into the double-lift strop. Following Shep's opinion that 'there's something terribly wrong with this guy, boss' I suggested that we dump him on to the lifeboat and call it a day. We would have looked pretty silly had we got called to a real rescue and had to carry it out with a madman lose in the cabin. It wasn't until we landed back at base that we discovered that our 'madman' wasn't the assigned casualty at all, but simply a drunk who'd either fallen or jumped into the harbour just before we'd arrived. Soon after we'd left him in the care of the lifeboat crew his condition had deteriorated further, and an ambulance had been called. So we called that Strike Three.

An hour later we were airborne again for another demonstration, this time in the River Helford, just two minutes to the south of us. But in those two minutes we got another call from the coastguard to divert to the rocks at Porthallow beach, again only nearby, where a 40-year-old man, ironically from Hayle, was stranded on a ledge with his fishing gear. The post-flight reports were starting to become rather brief.

Diver lowered and double lift carried out. Diver lowered again and recovered angling gear. Casualty flown to field at top of cliffs and deposited.

Strike Four.

Back to the Helford River for the demo, but no, another diversion to Porthscathoe where two persons were stuck on a cliff. Again from the report:

Rescue 23 proceeded to Porthscathoe and arrived at 1610. Observed that the two persons had made their way to the top of the cliffs. Five further people were seen at the bottom of the cliffs and Rescue 23 remained on scene until all were safely at the top. 23 then departed to carry out a demo at the Helford.

Strike Five.

Sunset wasn't due until 20.20 that evening and it had been the sort of hot day when people love to play in the water, so it was little surprise when yet another shout came in just as we were washing up the supper plates. Two kids had been reported drifting out to sea from the picturesque fishing village of Porthleven that was barely further from us than the end of the main runway. We scrambled at 18.53, airborne at 18.55 and on scene at 18.57. Sure enough there were two teenagers in an inflatable rubber dinghy, only a hundred metres off the entrance to the harbour, but paddling as hard as they could against the gentle offshore wind.

Lesson #2: *Never go out in an inflatable when the wind is blowing offshore.*

We lowered Scouse for a quick check that the boys were otherwise OK and, having established that they were fine, we simply hovered our way into the harbour entrance blowing the dinghy ahead of us. A quick thumbs-up from the boys and we high-tailed it back to the airfield. Strike Six.

It may not have been a particularly auspicious day of rescues and it was a bit doubtful whether some of them qualified for the term, but never the less we had been scrambled six times in one day and thereby smashed the previous record of four.

As we wearily descended the stairs to the car park I looked across at Shep and asked, 'Where are we going next?'

'Home, boss, it's time to go home.'

SUMMER DAYS, DOCTORS AND DISPLAYS

RESCUE FLYING IN THE SUMMER was always in stark contrast to the winter. The county of Cornwall in winter is not an appetising place to be. Cold winds stream in from the Atlantic while the seas are whipped up into huge rollers that boil when they hit the enormous cliffs. In these conditions it's not at all hard to imagine the days gone by of rum smugglers and shipwreck scavengers. No tourists made the trek to the south-west in the cold and wet months so in the winter we knew that call-outs would be few and far between. But summer time in Cornwall was an entirely different matter, and our six rescues in one day typified the month of August most years. With the weather generally fabulous, visitors would stream down to Devon and Cornwall in their thousands. The roads weren't designed to take caravans and the Cornish hedges hid solid stone walls that caused the early demise of many a towed home.

The days started amiably enough with a short 15-minute SAR test. Being holiday time, a skeleton crew of one air traffic controller and a single fire crew formally opened the airfield to allow us to have a quick look round and check that nothing was amiss with the huge acreage, the 2-kilometre main runway, and all the attendant hangars and support buildings. It was a tradition that was written somewhere into the air station manual but the real purpose was simply to give us a chance to warm up the duty SAR helicopter in preparation for events the day might throw at us. In practice we used the fifteen minutes to collect our breakfast: the untouched and heavily protected grass between the runways was a haven for the biggest and tastiest mushrooms you could ever imagine. It seemed crass to just land and pluck them so we pretended to ourselves that we were carrying out a valid training exercise by hovering over each mushroom and lowering our diver, Scouse, to accurately capture each 'casualty'. It's possibly the most expensive way to harvest mushrooms but it did sharpen us up, and sometimes more than intended. Shep and Scouse were my favourite crew team and many of the stories in this book are shared experiences with them. They were not only highly professional but also had the sharpest wit. If Shep ever lowered Scouse too quickly to the mushroom, or if Scouse ever forgot to dangle an earthing line to the ground first, then a massive electric shock of static would race up Scouse's body and leave him a jabbering and shaking wreck for several minutes. Much better to remind ourselves of that during the collection of breakfast than to do so halfway through a real rescue. With the mushroom casualties safely gathered, we would settle down to a fine breakfast feast of mushrooms on toast.

Occasionally there would be drownings or cliff fatalities, but by and large we could enjoy the work in good flying weather and there were plenty of opportunities to exercise our skills without too much stress or danger to ourselves. We would programme in a flight for a Search and Rescue Exercise, or SAREX, each day but this was

I found a masseur with sufficient skill to straighten out my spine and spare me the continuous pain. In all other medical regards we were encouraged never to self-medicate, and to be constantly aware of whether or not we were fit to fly. Any number of minor complaints, such as flu or even just cold, could upset the balance system enough to render a pilot a danger to himself and to others. Thus it was that I found myself at the airfield sick bay one morning complaining of a little constipation. I was ushered into the office of a brand new doctor who had qualified only a few weeks earlier. On completion of the examination I offered my prescription to the medic at the dispensary window. 'Are you pregnant, sir?' he politely enquired. On receiving the response that it was pretty unlikely he excused himself to check the prescription with the young doctor. Back he came a moment later with the observation that my prescription was an unusual way of treating constipation but who was he, a lowly petty officer, to argue with an officer? I wasn't to find out until the next day that I had been prescribed Maxalon, a drug designed to cure morning sickness during pregnancy, and had been allocated ten times the normal dose. The junior doctor's theory was that if it relaxed the stomach then it might cure constipation. I thanked the PO and set off to the squadron in good time for our midday duty start.

As luck would have it we had a couple of shouts almost immediately and so it was supper time before I remembered that I was supposed to take a pill with every meal. It was a fine and still summer's evening but had turned a little cold and we could be pretty confident that there would be no more flying trade for us in the hour remaining before darkness. The tourists would all be safely tucked up in the pub by now. We settled down to a final hour of watching the TV and I was more than entertained to see pink alligators climbing up the curtains next to the small black and white set. I did mention to Scouse that I wasn't feeling very well but by that time there were only a few minutes of duty time left so I braved it out.

The drive home was a trip in more ways than one. By the time I pulled into the driveway I had to honk the horn to get my wife to come and help me out of the car. I curled up in bed while she phoned the sick bay only to receive the classic naval medical advice: 'Take two aspirins, go to bed, and come and see me in the morning.' An hour later and I was in a pretty bad way. All my muscles were trying to contract at the same time with the result that I was curled up in a foetal position. Another call to the sick bay thankfully reached one of the regular and very senior doctors who normally ran the place. On hearing the odd symptoms the doctor suggested that my wife drove me back to the station for a proper examination. It was no small task to get me back into the car but only a five-minute drive to the base. The regular doctor took one look at me in the car and immediately ordered an ambulance to take me to Treliske, the main Cornish hospital that I was more used to visiting by air. (Had it been daylight, that's exactly how he would have had me transported.) Instead you have to imagine what it would be like to take a hair-raising 30-minute ride in an ambulance with lights and sirens going, while taking a bad trip on LSD. Each turn of the blue light reflected eerily into the back of the vehicle and apparently I found each lurch around a tight corner hysterically funny.

At Treliske they pumped my stomach and kept me in for observation overnight. By the morning I was fine again and I was able to return to flying just a couple of days later. From that day forward I never bought my own drink again if the junior doctor was in the Culdrose Wardroom, and I retain a lifelong mistrust of taking any form of pill. When asked to fill out forms asking about whether I have a known allergic reaction to any drugs I of course write 'Maxalon'. The inevitable response from doctors and nurses is: 'How on earth do you even know that?' and so it's a story I've had to tell many times.

The great summer event for us at Culdrose was the Air Day. Most operational airbases love to put on a show to the public: it sharpens up all the aviators, gives the public the opportunity to see the expensive hardware they're funding and generates income for deserving local charities. The event at Culdrose was particularly worth seeing for several reasons: we had more helicopters than at any other base in Europe, the Navy at that time had a good selection of fast, powerful and noisy jets, and there were never any noise complaints as the local populace recognised the value of having the base nearby. In fact, the majority were serving in the Navy, married to someone who was, or earned their living from the airbase.

Each different type of helicopter would perform a display that was suitable for their size and role but a highlight was the 'flutterby', when every helicopter that could possibly be made to fly would stream overhead in the biggest formation you were ever likely to see. Flying in formation is a demanding task in a helicopter. In a fixed-wing aircraft, regardless of the speed it flies at, a light touch on the airframe next to you could often be survived as there's very little relative movement; it would be like touching door handles on two fast cars running in the same direction. But the tips of the rotor blades on a helicopter are rotating at something close to the speed of sound, and the returning rotors on the helicopter next to you are travelling in the opposite direction, so a touch of two rotor blades would be catastrophic. The rule was therefore to space ourselves at two and a half rotor spans from each other.

Each squadron would first gather together in their own formation consisting of around a dozen helicopters. Leading the group was relatively easy as you just had to fly smoothly, at accurate speed and make any turn a wide and gentle event. At the back of the formation it was a tougher task as you had to match the movements of all the ones in front. The second and third rows in their many corrections to keep in formation would be inducing successively increasing movements up and down until it became like a roller coaster at the back. If, additionally, you were on the outside of the formation, it was necessary to greatly reduce the speed on the inside of a turn and accelerate to high speeds on the outside of a turn. Once the CO at the front levelled out from the turn you needed to decelerate fast before you ran into the guy in front of you. Another difficult place to be was in the middle of a diamond formation with helicopters on every side of you. Of course, any squadron consisted of varying levels of pilotage skills and you would always check out who was scheduled to be alongside. The leader was the only one who had an easy time of it.

Each squadron practised independently in the preceding weeks and as it was something we didn't do very often most of us were rusty at the outset. By the time Air Day arrived we were doing it with less terror in our hearts and were looking pretty good. The dress rehearsal on the day before the event was the first time that all squadrons that year joined up together. This occupied a great deal of airspace as each independent formation lumbered around into a position where it could slot in behind the formation in front. The join-up point was about five miles on the extended centre line of the runway and it would take all of those five miles to get everybody organised into a pretty pattern. As we arrived overhead, everybody would simultaneously let off smoke. It was an impressive sight from the ground and made for great photographs – in which one could readily spot anybody who was incapable of judging two and a half rotor spans accurately.

Flutterbys all passed without incident during my time at Culdrose, but the day of the fleet review by Her Majesty the Queen on the occasion of her silver jubilee in 1977 produced a rather different result. An even bigger formation of machines from throughout all the navy bases had gathered for the big day and a mass practice for the day before was scheduled. The join-up point was over southern Hampshire, from where we would run up the Solent past the Needles lighthouse, along the impressive line-up of anchored warships and eventually over the top of the Royal Yacht *Britannia*. It was a tradition that went back to the days of Henry VIII (albeit without helicopters) and timing was everything. The plan had been made such that the huge stream of helicopters would arrive over *Britannia* at exactly the same time as the fast jets screamed overhead, about 500 feet higher. This would all have been fine if it were not for the vagaries of the English summer which produced un-forecast low cloud over the Solent just as we all arrived. Each squadron formation stuck it out for as long as they dared but flying in formation in cloud is not an activity to be recommended. One by one the COs cried chicken and peeled away out of the scudding clouds with little more than a prayer and an acute ear to the radio to prevent one squadron from running into the side of another. There was no single airfield capable of taking everybody on such a mass diversion from the plan and it took all of the next 24 hours to gather everybody back to their assigned departure points for the big day. The day itself still brought a pall of drizzle but passed without incident and it was a pleasure and a privilege to be a part of such a huge event.

Back at Culdrose the Air Days could also be relied upon to bring unpredictable weather, but it was a royal marine and not the weather that nearly caused my early demise. When the SAR and training outfit 771 Squadron upgraded from the single-engined Wessex Mark 1 to the powerful twin-engined Wessex Mark 5, we inherited the airframes from the 'Junglies', as we referred to the Commando Squadrons whose responsibility it was to deliver fighting forces into remote locations. It would be several months before all the airframes were repainted from their drab olive camouflage into the dark blue and dayglo orange that signified SAR. Thus it came about that I was flying a green Junglie Wessex on Air Day and had to take part in a mock assault scenario.

Many of the compatriots I had joined the Navy with had gone to Junglie training, but I had studied anti-submarine flying instead. Junglies had more fun and were a hardy bunch, often assigned to living and operating out of tents in the Arctic while the rest of us had nice warm cabins on aircraft carriers. HRH Prince Charles was a Junglie at around the same time and was highly regarded both as a pilot and a crewmate on the squadrons on which he served. Although I didn't have Junglie training, the basic techniques were pretty obvious and the task required flying with flare and gusto… all fine by me. The flutterby would be the culmination to the Air Day and so we all had smoke canisters fitted to our wheel struts, but first came the mock assault. My cabin was filled with fully kitted-out marines and my job was to deliver them in front of the crowd as part of a group of Junglies, just as the jets were dive-bombing the airfield and giving the armourers the opportunity to set off huge black explosions and frighten the kids.

We ran in as a formation, fast and low. As we crossed the airfield boundary we opened out the gap between each helicopter, then executed a massive flare to bring each machine to a shuddering halt in the sky. The trick was to execute the flare in such a way as to kiss the ground with the tail wheel, then rotate the rest of the helicopter around the tail wheel to bring the main wheels firmly into contact with the ground. At that point the crewman, in this case Detlef Wodak, would give a thumbs-up to the marines, who would smartly exit the aircraft cabin and throw themselves to the grass looking generally mean and war-like. The brief was to remain on the ground for no more than a few seconds, then pull to full power and climb away. Even in isolation it took some concentration but the act of doing it in a formation with a dozen other Junglies while attack jets were descending above us and explosions were going off beneath us added a bit of spice.

I was elated at the arrival and achieved a reasonable imitation of a Junglie landing in action. I called 'Go' to Detlef, the marines exited smartly and Detlef called 'Clear'. But as I hauled in full power and rotated the nose of the Wessex forwards to achieve maximum acceleration in formation with the others alongside us there was another cry from Detlef: 'Oh no!' The last marine out of the cabin had thought it a jolly good wheeze to pull the string that would ignite the smoke canister on our wheel. The act of pulling in the power had sent the airflow straight through the cabin and up into the cockpit, whereupon I went instantaneously blind. I don't mean I couldn't see ahead, I mean I couldn't see my instruments or windscreen, my whole world just went orange. It happened so fast and so unexpectedly that there was little I could do beyond continuing muscle actions that would take us along the pre-assigned flight path. If I slowed I would be run into by the guy behind. If I climbed I would be run into by the jets, and if I descended I would be taken out by the demonstration explosives going off beneath us. All I could do to help the situation was to lean my head as far out of the door as I could, not easy when you're firmly strapped into the seat, and try to peer through the thick and acrid orange smoke that was streaming past my helmet. Of course it felt like a lifetime but after about ten seconds the increased airspeed changed the flow of the smoke and it cleared from my cockpit as fast as it had appeared, enabling us to continue the climb in formation to join the next display.

The subsequent photos of the big formation fly-past are not quite as symmetrical as usual as just one Wessex is not streaming smoke. Detlef was still apoplectic when eventually we landed and re-grouped at the squadron and he went off to find the marine in question. I didn't like to ask how he had 'explained' to the marine the error of his ways, I was just happy to have survived another Air Day.

A PLEASANT SURPRISE

ONE DAY AN ADMIRAL CAME to Culdrose. I dusted off my dark blue suit, marched smartly towards him, saluted and shook his proffered hand. With his other he handed me a neatly rolled piece of paper in a bow. It read:

COMMENDATION

Lieutenant J. Grayson, Royal Navy

771 Naval Air Squadron

On 31 July, 1978 the duty Wessex 1 SAR crew from Royal Naval Air Station Culdrose was scrambled to the area of Trevose Head, North Cornwall to rescue four men trapped at the base of a 100 foot cliff.

The weather was poor with a 20 knot northerly wind, heavy rain and a cloud base level with the clifftop. On arrival at the scene the four men were found to be on a ledge just above the heavy surf, inside a small cove opening to the West.

Hovering the helicopter close to the cliff was extremely difficult as the downdraughts were severe and the cliff face vertical. Two attempts were made and, on the first occasion, the pilot, Lieutenant GRAYSON, had to initiate overshoot action, pulling full power to avoid being thrown against the cliffs. A successful hover was achieved with a reasonable power margin on the second attempt.

The diver, Leading Aircrewman GIBBS, was lowered and immediately began to spin at a fast rate due to strong air currents; this was only controlled when the winchman, Leading Aircrewman HARRIS quickly lowered the diver into the water. Leading Aircrewman GIBBS then swam through 10 foot high waves and heavy surf to reach the ledge. As he swam to the ledge the helicopter wash inched close to the cliff to lessen the bight on the inch wire.

After climbing on to the ledge, Leading Aircrewman GIBBS released the winch hook and a stretcher was lowered from the helicopter. Leading Aircrewman GIBBS then assessed the injuries and, after much difficulty, one injured man was stretcher-lifted to the helicopter and three shocked but uninjured men were double-lifted to the clifftop. The injured man was flown, in visibility of 1,000 metres and a cloud base of 150 feet to Truro Hospital.

I commend Lieutenant GRAYSON for the courage and professional skill which he displayed during this rescue.

Knight Commander of the Most Honourable Order of the Bath,
  Vice-Admiral in Her Majesty's Fleet and
  Flag Officer Naval Air Command

14 September 1978

So now I had something to stick into the section in my logbook marked 'Awards and Commendations', and this was something I had never expected to be able to do. I had always assumed it was a page for other people. There was no associated medal or ribbon to be worn but the real significance to me lay in the fact that (as I only then found out) 'H' Harris had landed from that sortie and gone to see the CO with the SAR report clutched in his hand and the suggestion that I ought to receive some form of recognition for the flight I'd just flown. The CO had listened to the story, submitted a recommendation and, hey presto, I was now the recipient of an Admiral's Commendation. That one of these hard-bitten matelots from a team that prided itself on nonchalance had seen fit to do this affected me greatly. It was high praise, and I was quietly very proud indeed.

A BAD DECISION

NOT ALL OF OUR SCRAMBLES HAD fortunate endings and some would stay with me for years afterwards. I very clearly remember my first 'stiff' – a Frenchman on holiday with his family. Too much wine for lunch, got a bit out of his depth and spent a good half hour on the bottom of the bay before anybody thought to call us. I don't think I'd ever seen a dead body up close before, but I happened to glance down as the diver came up on the winch with his sad cargo and, just for a moment, I looked straight into the lifeless eyes.

Nothing much was said between us on the way to Treliske hospital. The boys in the back weren't qualified to certify a man dead so they had to continue with resuscitation techniques on even the most unlikely victims. I was often in a hurry to get to the hospital to avoid putting my team through any more pain. As we bumped on to the grass playing fields there would inevitably be a doctor waiting for us and a nurse with defibrillation paddles primed and ready to go, in case something could be done.

The pilot is lucky. He's separated from most of the traumatic aspects of a rescue while the diver and the crewman have to go through experiences that must haunt them for a long time afterwards. In extreme cases they would remove their intercom microphones to separate me further from their activities down in the cabin.

On our return from the Frenchman job I was unsure how to play it with the boys. They didn't say anything all the way back from Truro to Culdrose and I wasn't going to be the first to break the silence. These guys had been there and seen it all many times before and there was obviously an etiquette to be observed, I just wasn't sure yet what it was. We secured the aircraft in silence and as we walked back to the crewroom together the meal wagon arrived. As usual we set about supper like wolves. Still nobody had said anything until suddenly, just as I was raising the second mouthful of steak and chips, the diver blurted out to the crewman some particularly unpleasant detail of the rescue. I slowly lowered the fork and pushed the plate away before excusing myself to do some paperwork in the other office. 'Oh, not eating, boss? Can I have your chips?'

I soon learned to harden up. There was to be no sparing of the pilot's sensibilities once we were on the ground. We either did things as a team or we didn't do them at all.

The divers had all trained as crewmen and then gone on to learn their particular specialisation. It was a tough course and they were as fit as athletes. Pete Gibbs, one of our favourite divers, and several of the others had served on the Field Gun Crew in the annual display of teamwork at Earl's Court. They trained together for months before the opening of the Royal Tournament. It was a gruelling job and many of them severely damaged limbs while hauling the iron barrels of ancient field guns across the wall, through the gap and over 'the ravine'. It was a matter of extreme pride each year as to which of the three teams won the tournament: Plymouth Naval

Base, Portsmouth Naval Base and the Fleet Air Arm crew. I have it in mind that we usually won but I can't be certain.

It was the diver who would have to put his life on the line time and time again. They never complained about danger; they would only rant if somebody had been particularly stupid. In the middle of 1979 they had good cause to complain and we all joined in with them. Word had come down from somewhere way on high that we were no longer going to have divers at all. I've no idea where this came from and I'm not about to start blaming the RAF, though it's true to say that the idea originated from the fact that we had divers and they didn't. This wasn't surprising; we operated from ships and around coastlines, while they operated from airfields that were often inland. We had each developed slightly different techniques to suit our field of operations. The RAF were, for example, unsurpassed in mountain rescue. Their Search and Rescue crews at Brawdy, Valley, Leuchars and Kinloss were regularly tasked into the Brecon Beacons, Snowdonia, the Cairngorms and the Isle of Skye. They were hot cookies at finding their way up a mountain pass in a zero-visibility blizzard, picking up a party of lost hikers and finding their way back down again. I wouldn't have liked to do it. We were good around the cliffs but I always had the luxury of a relatively flat seascape to descend to and find my way home from.

A yellow RAF machine arriving in a snowstorm with a diver dressed in a wetsuit would, I assume, have been less prepared than had they arrived with a trained and suitably attired mountaineer. On the other hand, it would not be sensible for a blue-and-dayglo Navy machine to arrive at the scene of a ditched aircraft with a mountaineer all dressed and ready to go. This seemed to us to be a pretty straightforward argument at the time, but sometimes the logic flies out of the window when funding cuts are sought. Decades of incompetent procurement had lead to the extraordinary set of circumstances where a pencil that could be bought from WHSmith for something under a pound would cost the armed services over £70 by the time it had gone through the system. Cuts had to be made and we were an obvious target when our crews cost more to train than an RAF crew.

It's not generally appreciated that the Navy and the RAF never set out to provide a service to civilians. We each stationed helicopters at our airbases purely and simply to recover fixed-wing aircrew who got into difficulties and had to abandon their aircraft. Over a period of time the airbases would receive requests for assistance and, of course, they would do everything they could to help. As military air crashes came less and less frequently, so the civilian tasking increased. It was good practice for the crews, good PR for the local airbase and an efficient use of humanitarian resources. But it was a long time before the changing roles were recognised and the Department of Trade and Industry allocated extra funding to the military to help with this growing responsibility.

Inevitably much of our work in Cornwall was along beaches, up the sides of cliffs and sometimes even inland, but we were still a naval unit and our divers were invaluable. An RAF crewman was not allowed to disconnect himself from the winch and swim around in the water. He had to swing past the survivor and try to grab him from the safety of his harness. This was assuming that the victim was on the surface. The Navy's experience had taught us otherwise in our particular theatre of operations. In the early days of the big aircraft carriers we had regularly lost fixed-wing aircraft over the edge. They would try to overshoot from a poor approach, the engine would fail to spool up quickly enough and they'd wallow off the front of the ship into the water. We had therefore devised a system whereby the crewman stayed in the helicopter while the diver jumped from the open door with his breathing equipment and set off alone to find the survivors. Once he had brought them to the surface, attached them to his harness and was ready to go, he would give us the thumbs-up, we'd move over the top, he'd clip himself on together with his survivor and up they both would come. We'd been doing it that way for a very long time and our divers were the best in the world.

All of this seemed to go right over the heads of our lords and masters in the ministry who refused to be swayed by increasingly vociferous complaints from us that this decision could only lead to tragedy. In the last few days before the divers left the squadron we became more and more agitated. Letters were written to the captain saying things like: 'People will die as a direct result of this decision. It's not a question of whether, it's only a question of when.' We were met by a wall of silence. On 29 July 1979 the last of our divers left the squadron; on 30 July two people died.

It was a really fine day, bright blue skies, fluffy white clouds and a warm summer breeze. It would be a perfect day for the start of the Tall Ships race from Fowey on the south coast. Dozens of beautiful old ships, many of them crewed by under-privileged or handicapped children, glided majestically out of the harbour. It's a fabulous spot and a perfect harbour. Surrounded on all sides by a steep-sided and wooded valley, the water is calm, protected and deep. It has, for centuries, been the spot where coastal ships tie up to receive their cargo of china clay from the massive and ancient workings that extend for miles around. The tall white artificial mountains form a unique landscape that's often used by film companies to represent the surface of another planet. The rivers and streams that wind through the area carry a milky-white cocktail that flows out into St Austell bay. It has the effect of turning the water a stunning shade of light blue.

As their crews climbed into the rigging and unfurled enormous billowing sails, the ships slowly made their way past the castle and out to the start line off Gribben Head. They were accompanied by a large flotilla of local boats and some from much further afield. It was a prestigious event; the schools were on holiday and Cornwall was already full of holiday-makers taking advantage of the warmest climate in the UK.

Back at Culdrose it was a very quiet day, although we had already been airborne twice on routine tasks. As the duty SAR crew we were pretty autonomous. It was up to us to practise the things we hadn't done for a while and on this occasion we took ourselves down the Helford River and out into Falmouth Bay to practise with the grappling hook, a four-pronged, anchor-like affair that was attached to the end of the winch line and used to capture the various items of detritus we'd often find around the coast. Sometimes we'd find an old life raft and need to haul it up to try to identify its origin. At other times we behaved more like jackdaws, picking at shiny things that took our fancy. Our collection of escaped marker buoys was among the finest in the land. On special occasions we'd find something really useful. Our best day was when one of the crews stumbled upon an entire container floating just beneath the surface. The doors were open and a steady stream of brand new parka jackets floated to the surface. Half of Cornwall were wearing parkas by the end of the week; our squadron children's charity benefited handsomely and we'd all become world experts in rapid recovery techniques. The Cornish salvage tradition in a modern guise.

It had become obvious to us that we'd be needing the grapple hook even more these days. Without a diver we were going to have to forget many of the techniques we'd learned over the years and try to compensate for them in some way. Leading Aircrewmen Steve Wooley and John Boulton repeatedly hauled the hook in with our practice buoy attached, threw it out and tried again as I circled back to the start position. It was quite a fun exercise but our collective heart wasn't really in it. Being without a diver was like losing a limb and we were very, very nervous.

At 10.50 we were scrambled to Gribben Head. Polruan Coastguard had reported a light aircraft ditched half a mile out to sea. We always used the expression 'scrambled', although on this occasion we were simply diverted from the activity we were on. They still played the scramble tones over the tannoy back at Culdrose, in order to alert doctors, fire crews and any other specialists who might be required along the way. As chance would have it my old diver Jamie Bauld had come into the air station that morning and was standing in line at the pay office to sort out his final paperwork before leaving to go to some mind-numbing desk job. Like everybody else on the air station he heard the scramble tones and subsequent announcement but, unlike everybody else, he understood the significance. The duty SAR didn't have a diver on board. An aircraft was in the water; a diver would be required. It was as simple as that.

Jamie flew out of the pay office, jumped into his car and hurtled back to 771 where Andy Halliday, the senior SAR pilot and a Canadian of few words, was wringing his hands at the futility of the situation. The place lit up as Jamie arrived and both Andy and his crewman Gordon Rae leapt for the standby aircraft while Jamie threw his wetsuit and diving gear into the rear cabin door. No sooner had his feet left the ground than Andy hauled the machine into the air and set off in pursuit of us. They'd moved at lightning speed but they were already fifteen minutes behind us.

A small boat waved frantically to us as we scanned the scene on arrival. We could see they had a young boy on deck and were trying to resuscitate him. Just off to one side of the boat we could see the outline of the light aircraft lying just beneath the surface. One day earlier and I would have despatched the diver straight into the water from a hover height of around 20 feet. Today I didn't have a diver. If there were other survivors left in the aircraft there was absolutely nothing I could do about it. I called the situation to another old mate, Jerry English, who had arrived in an anti-submarine Sea King which had been practising near us in Falmouth Bay and had come with us to the scene. While Steve, John and I went into the hover over the small

boat and collected the young boy, Jerry's crew spotted two adults as they burst to the surface and quickly went in to pick them up.

The young lad we now had on board was clearly not in a good state. He was only semi-conscious and the boys had started to administer oxygen from the tanks we carried in the cabin. Happy that Jerry English was dealing with the other survivors, I set off to Treliske Hospital. We would learn later that Jerry had collected the light aircraft pilot and a Dutch photographer who had been hired to photograph the start of the race. The young boy I had aboard was one of two brothers, the sons of an executive from Lancia Cars who had sponsored one of the race boats. We didn't know it at the time but his brother was still trapped in the cockpit breathing stale air from a small trapped bubble. Even if we'd known we would have been powerless to help him.

Five minutes after we had departed to the hospital Andy Halliday arrived at the scene with Jamie sitting ready in the back door. He'd changed out of his civvies and was booted and spurred. As Andy hauled the nose up to bring the big Wessex to a shuddering halt, Jamie leapt from the door. The divers always went in feet first, holding their mask, then surfaced briefly to give us a thumbs-up before disappearing again. It was a pretty powerful impact they suffered each time they hit the water and we needed to know they were in control of the situation. Jamie quickly found the aircraft in about 60 feet of water. It must have been slowly sinking and rolling ever since the others had made their escape as, by now, it was inverted and had reached the bottom. In the back of the aircraft he found the other boy trapped by a seat belt that had caught one of his legs as the aircraft sank. It was clear that he'd been able to sustain himself by forcing his head into a small pocket of air that had remained in the cockpit. By the time Jamie reached him the air had all gone and Jamie still had to get him up though 60 feet of ocean.

The two men survived but, three hours after Jamie's brave efforts, the young boy lost his battle for life. His brother was transferred to Papworth Hospital in Cambridge where sadly, three weeks later, he also died.

Every one of us was livid by the time we landed back at Culdrose. I can't remember the precise sequence of events because it was all seen through a red mist at the time. By eight o'clock the next morning our divers, every single one of them, had been returned to the squadron. Nobody ever said sorry. Nobody ever resigned or took the blame for such a truly awful piece of resource management. I just hope that the boys' family could take solace from the fact that their deaths were truly not in vain. I always intended to tell them myself but just a few days later (as we would shortly discover) we were in a major battle for our own lives and, somehow, I never quite got around to it. I wouldn't like to begin to count the number of lives that have since been saved as a direct result of the Navy keeping SAR divers; it will be many hundreds.

A COW CALLED JERRY

AMID THE INEVITABLE TRAGIC EVENTS of Search and Rescue there was also a great deal of laughter. We rarely allowed the morbid aspects of the job to get to us and there was much to keep us distracted.

As in a football or rugby team, as sailors we would rarely address one another by our real names. A sailor is called 'Jack', short for Jolly Jack Tar, by every other sailor, right up until he learns his real name. To attract the attention of another sailor you simply shout, 'Oi, Jack.' And when you did learn the 'real' name it was inevitably replaced by a nickname. We had 'Topsy' Turner, 'Shep' Woolley, 'Smiler' Grinney, 'Wally' Wallace and so on. The real name wasn't relevant, but once in a while you might discover it by accident while filling out an official form or something.

'Oi, Scouse, what initial shall I put on this wanky form?'

'It's L.'

'L? Nobody's got an initial L, that's a nancy sort of initial. What's it stand for then?'

'Nothin'.'

'It can't be nothin, that'd be an N, you dimwit.'

'It's Lawrence.'

At this point the whole crewroom erupted into gales of laughter. It was inconceivable that this lean mean scouse diver with a face like a boxer could possibly have been christened 'Lawrence'. He was ribbed mercilessly and continuously until the scramble tones went off or until something even funnier happened. Twenty-four hours later we'd all have forgotten, so that when it came up again it was just as funny as the first time.

If it was the real Navy then I, as an officer, would have addressed my crewman as Leading Aircrewman Woolley. He would salute smartly and address me as Sir. But it wasn't the real Navy, thank God. The thought of having that sort of exchange with Shep Woolley makes me giggle just to think of it. But one of us had to sign for the aircraft and one of us had to take the flack when we'd screwed up, so the pilot was always known as 'Boss'. The advantage of short sharp nicknames was that you didn't waste valuable time on the intercom pronouncing double-barrelled mouthfuls. Use a man's full title in the middle of a rescue and, by the time you'd got it all out, somebody would probably be dead.

We were visited one morning by the First Sea Lord Admiral Sir Henry Leach GCB, Commander in Chief of the Fleet. He'd requested to come flying and to experience an average morning with us, entirely without ceremony. This was just as difficult a request to fulfil as it would have been if the Queen had asked to drop by one day and help with the ironing. Sure enough he turned up at dawn in a goon suit marked 'CinC Fleet'. He joined us for scrambled eggs and rind-less rashers which Scouse had prepared in our tiny kitchen, until it was time for the morning SAR test.

He really enjoyed the flight and wanted to try his hand at the controls which, despite not being an aviator, he handled rather well. Afterwards he took the trouble to write a very charming thank-you letter and his visit had clearly been a great success. However, mid-flight I made a mistake that would haunt me for the weeks that followed. Relieved and overcome with the perfect weather conditions, and for want of conversation suitable for an admiral, I had muttered something like, 'It's mornings like this that make you glad to be alive, isn't it, sir?' I heard some strangling noises from down in the cabin before Shep and Scouse pulled their intercoms out of their sockets in order to avoid embarrassment with their laughter. It would be several weeks before I could walk past anybody in the corridor without having a brief burst of poetry quoted at me.

Sometimes even the rescues themselves offered opportunities for enjoyment, if they were simple and offered no danger to life or limb. We might have hoped for bikini-clad damsels in mild distress but they were few and far between, however. It's usually the male of the species who gets himself into a tight spot through bravado. One typical afternoon we were called to pick up two teenage boys who had managed to get themselves stuck halfway up a 200-foot cliff face. Most of the cliff faces in Cornwall are sheer. This one was unusual in that it was at a slight angle and had vegetation growing up it.

We had only just finished picking up a fifty-year-old gentleman from the upturned hull of his dinghy and were in the process of landing him on the beach. Normally this would be an opportunity for the diver to swagger around the beach for a couple of minutes chatting up the local talent and looking serious and macho, while the crewman and I stayed airborne to avoid chopping up enthusiastic children with our tail rotor. However, this time we touched our wheels briefly on the sand at Prussia Cove, unceremoniously left the survivor and headed off at top speed to Lantic Bay. The coastguards had been to the incident and decided that a helicopter would be the safest bet to rescue the two boys. It's worth noting at this point that the coastguards would deal with dozens of incidents a day during the summer months and we often worked together with great mutual respect. The boys' exploration had led them to a peculiar position under an overhang of cliff and they were tiring rapidly. It was a long way to the bottom if they let go.

I brought the aircraft into a hover, settled into my seat and started to move slowly in to the cliff face under the guidance of Gordon Rae. My regular crew were taking a well-earned rest after a continuous three-day rescue operation (which I will describe shortly) so Ritchie Burnett was the diver. Our biggest concern was to get Ritchie into a position from where he could get to the boys without our downwash blowing all three of them on to the rocks below. A Wessex at full power has no remorse for anything that lies beneath. We realised we were going to have to put Ritchie out on a very long line, and this would mean hovering with the tips of our rotor blades no more than eighteen inches from the rock face. This wouldn't be a problem for a well worked-up crew but I'd only been with Gordon for 48 hours and we hadn't yet had time to discover each other's limitations. It was therefore with some trepidation that I hovered slowly sideways under his voice commands.

We were in place. I locked my head into a completely static position looking out to the right of the aircraft. Provided I didn't set the ear canals moving and that I visually lined up a piece of the window with a piece of the rock face I could be reasonably confident of keeping the aircraft in a decent hover while Gordon shifted his attention to lowering Ritchie down to the terrified boys. As Ritchie swung back and forth in an attempt to get under the overhang I caught sight of something very peculiar at the edge of my peripheral vision. On the left-hand side of the aircraft I caught a fleeting impression of something red. I knew that in that direction lay only the sea and the sky, and usually these are both blue. There was no way I could have turned my head to get a better look, however, or we'd have joined Ritchie on the rocks beneath us and the coroner would be filling out forms for five of us.

Gordon was doing a great job with his continuous patter of information and I was making tiny muscle movements to adjust our position one inch that way and then two inches the other. Up came one of the boys clasped firmly between Ritchie's thighs in the double-lift harness. No sooner did we have him on board than Gordon was lowering Ritchie back down on the winch again. Ninety-nine per cent of my brain was concentrating on the job in hand, it had to be, but that last one per cent was working overtime trying to decode what it was I'd seen. I was hovering a long way up a cliff face, right side towards the cliff, left side out to sea. Anything on my left side therefore had to be airborne. If it was an aircraft then I didn't have a problem but I was certain that it had been much closer than that. My little one per cent went through a list of possibilities until I had narrowed it down to only two candidates: either I'd blown a piece of debris from the cliff face or something had worked loose and departed from my aircraft. The debris gave me more concern than the possibility of losing a bit of the aircraft. One piece of debris meant the possibility of more and it only takes a small plastic bag lodged in the wrong place to bring millions of pounds worth of helicopter out of the sky. If anything important had fallen off the aircraft, however, I would have known about it straight away through my hands.

Whatever it was, at this point I could do absolutely nothing about it. Gordon brought Ritchie and the second of his survivors away from the cliff face and up towards the door. As soon as he'd hauled them both inside he returned his full attention to our proximity to the cliffs and began to give me instructions to manoeuvre our way clear. There's a wonderful sensation that goes through every muscle in your body as you allow them to relax a little, one at a time. I've often thought that the street entertainers who mimic statues would make great rescue pilots. As sensation came back into my fingers, toes and middle spine I looked down through my open window for a clue as to what the red flash might possibly have been. I didn't need the eyes of a hawk to spot the culprit. At the bottom of the cliff, impaled on the sharp rocks, was a very flat red car. Gordon and Ritchie were busy checking out our survivors in the cabin when I interrupted them with: 'Umm, chaps, sorry to bother you, but does anyone know where that car came from?'

We landed the boys on the clifftop, handed them into the care of the coastguards, their parents and the small crowd that had gathered. It would take a few phone calls and a read of the newspapers the next day before we would learn the full story. I'll quote straight from the *Sunday Express*:

> *There was no hesitation for Stephen Rescorie when a call went out for help in saving two boys stranded on a cliff. Stephen, a 24 year old building worker, of Pelynt, Cornwall was visiting his girlfriend Mary Rose Taylor at her home in Polruan. Mary's father Basil is a local coastguard. Stephen said 'It was the natural thing to do to offer to take two coastguards up to the clifftop when the alarm was raised. I ran down the cliff towards the edge with them and I thought I'd put the handbrake on but maybe I didn't. On Tuesday insurance assessors will examine the car, which was comprehensively covered. The National Trust have asked that it be removed. Stephen said the Marina 1.8, which had cost him £1,700 four years ago had been doing about 60 miles an hour when it overtook him and plunged over the edge, narrowly missing a helicopter.*

Even at 60mph the car must have only just achieved enough momentum to clear our rotor blades. I don't like to dwell too long on the consequences if it hadn't.

Above Ten months old. Mum wrote, 'Admiral of the Fleet in his sailor suit'. I have obviously under-achieved!

Below left On the steps of the caravan I was born in.

Below right In front of one of the training Whirlwind 7s, 705 Squadron, with a very proud Mum after the ceremony of receiving our wings.

Above On HMS *Ark Royal* we thought we were a big ship, with around 2,500 men and 38 aircraft, but alongside the nuclear-powered USS *Nimitz* in Norfolk Naval Base, Virginia, we were dwarfed during our annual visits. (Photo: US Navy)

Above Hovering alongside the mighty *Ark* as we all wait for fixed-wing flying operations to begin for the day. (Photo: US Navy)

Below left When big green waves started breaking over the bows of an aircraft carrier you knew you were in for a rough night, but it was nothing compared to the day of Fastnet '79.

Below right I had hovered next to that helicopter for several hours as she fought to stay afloat, but in the end the battle was lost. To catch fire on the crane was the final ignominy.

Above At the height of the Cold War, flying the Wessex 1. F4 Phantoms parked on the deck of *Ark Royal* in the foreground, and a Russian warship, a Kresta II Class Cruiser called the *Admiral Makarov*, shadowed our every move just off to our stern.

Below With smoke still pouring from the cockpit I am flying completely blind during an air display joke that went dangerously wrong.

Above My diver, in his orange wetsuit, and crewman sitting with their feet out of the cabin door as we fly a coastal patrol, imprinting every inch of the towering Cornish cliffs into our memory banks.

Below Every new pilot had to earn the trust of his crew by balancing both wheels on the wall of a disused tin mine. It was the pinnacle of teamwork and required all three of us to be at the very top of our game.

Above 'Smiler' Grinney plays to camera while waiting on the slippery deck of a nuclear submarine. Down below 'Doc' Morgan is in a hurry to collect a very sick American sailor before the sub is obliged to dive.

Below Balancing one wheel on the 'Camel's Head'.

Above Fastnet 1979. After four straight hours in the saddle it's time for a 'hot' refuel and crew change. No time for posing and the adrenalin is still on overload.

Below left Serving breakfast to the real Admiral of the Fleet, Admiral Sir Henry Leach GCB, both in our goon suits, before going flying together.

Below right Checking out of the beaches on our way home from six rescues in one day.

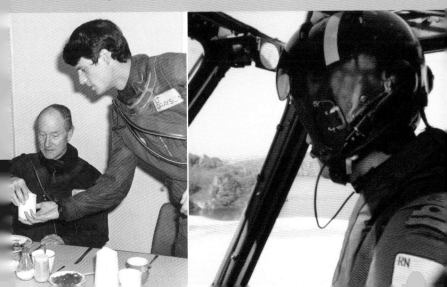

Above left On the steps of Buckingham Palace in March 1981 with Mum and my (then) wife Charlotte, who had put up with my long months away at sea and an alarm clock that went off at 3.30 most mornings when I was at home

Above right My Air Force Cross. A confusing name when awarded in the Royal Navy, but it has applied across all military aviators since the Second World War.

Below I am in two minds as to whether death in a scrapyard or life in a paintball venue is best for an old friend who was heroic in her own right. I guess the latter since I can one day go back and see her. This one served on Fastnet. (Photo: Gunsmoke Paintball)

And from the *Western Morning News* that week:

One of the rescued boys, Matthew Pickering said, 'We thought we'd had it but that pilot was an ace.'

Now you would think that gaining the nickname 'Ace' Grayson would be pretty cool. Not a chance. Ten days later a local farmer found one of his cows at the bottom of a small cliff. The animal had fallen over the edge and there was no way up. We took a vet, lowered a net, lowered the vet, watched him walk the cow on to the net, stun the cow, then we moved in and picked them all up. We landed our confused cargo on the grass and it went on to live a happy and presumably fulfilling life. The farmer and his wife were so grateful that they felt it necessary to express their gratitude to the local television station by announcing that, henceforth, the cow would be known in the herd as 'Jerry Ace Grayson'.

'WHAT RACE?'

MY ALTERCATION WITH A FLYING Morris Marina had come only three days after the end of the most significant rescue exercise ever carried out at Culdrose. The media at the time called it the 'most intensive rescue operation in maritime history'. The lessons learned during these three intensive days would lead to a complete rethink in the design of all ocean-going yachts, and the name of a tiny rocky outcrop off southern Ireland would cement itself in the history books. The name was Fastnet.

It was the middle of summer. The Royal Naval Air Station at Culdrose was effectively closed as the Navy tried to acknowledge that their employees had wives, children and a life beyond wearing a blue suit. You accept, when you join, that leave is a privilege, not a right. The Navy trains you, the Navy pays you, the Navy owns you, but at some point in the past they had realised that if married men were to be sent to sea for months at a time they had to be given the chance to spend time with their families when they were ashore. Culdrose is the biggest helicopter base in Europe and, as such, it's home to many different squadrons. There are initial training squadrons, operational training squadrons, 'second line' squadrons conducting various trials, and front-line squadrons who go to sea. Then there are all the support departments to administer the domestic side of running such a large organisation. There was no hope of ever coordinating the holidays of three thousand men and women when they all wanted to take time off during the school summer holidays so the place just shut down for three weeks and left the bare essentials running, including us. We used to joke that if you wanted to invade the UK it would be a good idea to do it on a Wednesday afternoon in August: the Navy were on holiday and the RAF had their mid-week sports afternoon.

We loved this time on the SAR team. We kept up our usual routine and we had the whole airfield to ourselves. When we were on the ground we didn't have to pretend we were also naval officers with reports to write and training exercises to run, we just lounged around – and we were pretty good at that. The duty crew could often be found asleep in the sunshine or, if we felt particularly energetic, we'd all wash our cars until it was either time to eat or to watch the TV news. Little did we know that Kate Adie would soon be filing her hourly news reports from our own tiny crewroom. But we always knew the quickest route to the helicopter and we were regularly pushing our scramble times below the 90-second base mark.

Of course, an English summer is never quite as fine as it ought to be and, although it was warm, the holidaymakers weren't having much fun on 9 August 1979 as a small tropical storm with 70 mph winds scythed a path of havoc across the country. We scrambled to a cabin cruiser named the *Zanadu*, which began taking on water when three portholes were smashed, 12 miles off Plymouth. We accompanied the boat all the way into harbour but our winch stayed firmly in its housing and the family on board suffered only a big fright and a little discomfort. Elsewhere various people were picked up by lifeboats around the coast and no lives were lost. The storm abated as quickly as it had arrived, just in time for me and my crew to enjoy our scheduled three days off.

Although we worked a regular routine, it was a schedule the body's natural clock didn't like at all. We'd start at dawn for three mornings and work till midday, then work four afternoons till dusk, then have three days off. Next we'd have four mornings, three afternoons and four days off before starting the routine again. It was a good way of coping with summer days that started at 3am and finished at 10.30pm, but the constant change over three years would eventually give me a massive stomach ulcer.

We came back to work on the morning of the thirteenth but it turned out to be a quiet day. We launched at about nine for a quick check of the airfield and surrounding area but the visibility was beginning to deteriorate and we didn't feel like stretching ourselves when everyone else was on holiday. Even the standby crew would stay at home in August. We would prepare their aircraft for them and they would stay near a phone. Whenever we went a long way from base our resident coastguard would phone around the boys, who could be in and dressed within a few minutes. We lounged professionally for the remainder of the morning and were ultimately surprised not to get any call-outs. By lunchtime we were home but the clouds were turning very dark.

As we came into work at 03.30 on the morning of Tuesday the fourteenth it was as if winter had arrived four months early. Trees were down across the road and dustbins were lying on their side. Dawn would arrive in an hour but the rain was horizontal and it would be a while before we really saw any daylight. Unusually I was first in through the swing doors on the ground level of the squadron office block, but I could hear that the coastguard telephone was already ringing upstairs. I took the stairs three at a time and found myself speaking to the Culdrose Air Officer of the Day. He was starting to receive calls from the rescue control centres at both Plymouth and Lands End. He had a very unclear picture so far but there were a number of reports of yachts aground on the Scilly Isles, about 40 minutes' flying time to the west of Culdrose. He asked that we get airborne as quickly as we could while he started to ring around to find some extra crews. He suspected that the overnight storm had caught out a number of yachts in the race and that we were going to have our work cut out. I innocently asked, 'What race?' and was met with disdain. I had no idea that the most prestigious event in the yachting calendar had departed from the Isle of Wight the previous Saturday afternoon.

The best yachtsmen in the world had gathered for Cowes Week and the Fastnet Race was the culmination of a week of racing. By the Monday they had cleared the south-west tip of Cornwall and made their way up towards Ireland. By around noon the leaders had rounded the Fastnet Rock and headed back towards Cornwall. The Radio 4 shipping forecast was giving 'South-westerly 4 or 5, increasing 6 or 7 for a time, veering westerly later'. Four hours later this was amended to include a warning of Gale Force 8 for the Fastnet area but most of the skippers had missed that broadcast. A further amendment, warning of an imminent severe force 9 gale, never made it to the BBC studio in time for the evening shipping forecast. Thus most of the fleet of 303 racing yachts had sailed on through Monday night believing that the weather was on their side. By halfway through the night it had reached storm force 10.

I leapt back down the stairs to tell the engineers to hurry their preparations, nearly knocking over our very experienced coastguard officer, Dick Harvey. Coming in the doors at the bottom of the stairway were my diver 'Smiler' Grinney and a new crewman, John Charnley. I refer to him as new because I'd never flown with him before but he was actually a superb instructor who was just filling in for one of the regulars. By the end of the day I would be eternally grateful that he was on our crew.

Very little was said as we each concentrated hard on ticking off our individual responsibilities. Getting airborne quickly is a good thing, getting airborne under-prepared is unforgivable and the only fear we knew well was that of letting down the rest of the crew. By 04.35 we were airborne and on our way to the Scillies. It was certainly a rough and bumpy ride but the visibility wasn't too bad and the cloud-base was nearly 1,000 feet. We still had no idea of the size of the racing fleet, nor of the scale of the storm that was raging about 80 miles north of us. As far as we were concerned, we were on our way to find either one or two abandoned yachts on the coast of the Scillies and maybe their crews huddled on the beach. We arrived at the little cluster of islands and began our visual search, far too low to pick up radio calls from Culdrose. We couldn't find anything and had only been there a short time when the local coastguard called us on the radio to say that the crew from the only definite incident had been found alive and well having breakfast in the local guest house. He ended the transmission with a request from Culdrose that we climb higher on our way home and establish early communications with them.

As we passed through 700 feet and our radio reception improved it seemed that the whole world had gone stark staring mad. Bearing in mind that it was still only 05.40 in the morning and that Culdrose was all on leave, I simply could not believe the sheer volume of radio chatter going on. It seemed that one helicopter after another was coming hurtling out of Culdrose, every one of them trying to speak at the same time, either to receive a briefing or to send new information. Meanwhile, on our coastguard emergency frequency there was complete bedlam as one yacht after another put out a Mayday call asking for immediate assistance. We had only been gone just over an hour and the weather didn't seem to be as severe as all that. Where, indeed, had the Air Officer of the Day found so many aircrew at that time of the morning? The more I listened the more I realised that there were only three other aircraft, they were just all talking at once and I was listening to two separate frequencies simultaneously. I quite literally couldn't believe my ears as all three of us in my aircraft strained to put a picture together. At 05.43 Culdrose issued a situation report, known universally as a SITREP. It consisted of:

Yacht MAGIC rudderless and shipping heavy seas.
Yacht GRIMALKIN 30 miles north west of Lands End, capsized.
Yacht TARANTULA sinking over 100 miles beyond the Scillies.
Yacht MULLIGATAWNY dismasted and in distress even further out.
Red flares sighted by yacht MORNING TOWN.
Four men sighted in a life raft by unknown yacht, and then lost to view.
Three yachts ashore on the Scillies, updated ten minutes later to five yachts.

I faced a serious dilemma. There was still another 20 minutes before I could make it back to Culdrose for fuel. Should I continue and top up my tanks or should I turn around and do what I could with the fuel remaining? We rarely flew with full tanks; it was simply too much weight to carry when we might find ourselves wanting to hover near the cliffs and needing enough power to do it. The Wessex Mark 5 is a very powerful helicopter but with a severe downdraught curling over the cliff edge it could still leave you short of lift. We measured power in terms of percentage; at 100 per cent you were about to run out. You could use a little extra for a few seconds but you were running the risk of blowing up the two big Rolls Royce jets that turned the rotors. It was usually only in the hover that you'd ever find yourself short of power; a helicopter loves to fly forwards and uses much less power to do that – maybe only 40 or 50 per cent of the power available. If we were going to be hovering out at sea in such a strong wind I knew I'd be able to take a full fuel load on board. We'd be hovering stationary over the water but in a 60 or 70 mph wind the helicopter would think it was flying forwards and therefore use a fraction of the power. My mind was made up as I was passed by a Sea King and then the standby Wessex flown by Albie Fox, both going in the opposite direction. The Sea King would head out to the very long-distance Maydays while Albie would start to deal with the more immediate problems closer to shore. There were over 20,000 square miles of ocean for us to deal with and I could hear on my radio that the RAF had launched a Nimrod from St Mawgan to coordinate and prioritise the various requirements. I would be far more useful with a full tank of fuel so I pressed on to Culdrose.

The ground crew, as ever, were superb. The big hose was already uncoiled and lying across the tarmac. All I had to do was accurately land on the spot and within seconds they would be pumping many gallons of Avtur aboard my aircraft. John Charnley supervised the refuelling while Smiler ran inside to try and get a better picture of what the hell was going on. Within minutes we were airborne again. There were now two Sea Kings attacking the problem and two Wessex. Broadly speaking, the Sea Kings were dealing with the area to the west of the Scillies while Albie and I headed north. The controller on the Nimrod was reeling off the names of yacht after yacht in difficulties: *Charioteer, Magic, Tarantula, Grimalkin, Bonaventure II, Trophy, Camargue, Hestrul II, Skidbladner, Ariadne, Gunslinger, Callirhoe III, Polar Bear, Anatomy* and so it went on. As we crossed the north Cornish coast I just kept shaking my head. I couldn't believe what was happening. In the little town of Helston the crews who hadn't gone away on holiday were waking up and hearing the BBC news. Anybody who'd stayed in Cornwall rushed straight into the airbase.

The seas to the north were incredible. I could only guess at what they must have looked like from the deck of a yacht; from where I was sitting in my relatively cosy cockpit it seemed that every wave was bigger than the last. We were all muttering expletives as giant rollers curled in from the Atlantic. My guess was that some were over 40 feet from crest to trough and the powerful wind was throwing a horizontal jet of spray from the top of every one. We stayed at a height of about 200 feet: if we went too high we'd suffer a reduction in speed as the wind increased; if we went too low we might pass a yacht and never spot it. Frankly we were having trouble putting a scale to the waves and thereby knowing what a yacht would actually look like. Your eyes are much more efficient if they know what to expect. Smiler was leaning out into the gale and wiping the salt from his eyes as he scanned the trough of every wave we passed. Even at 200 feet the rain had salt in it. John was carefully plotting our every move on his chart, noting our speed, noting any changes in our direction of travel and simultaneously trying to build up a picture of where the yachts in trouble might be in relation to our position.

On the emergency channel we heard a call; it seemed to be louder and clearer than the other calls. A plaintive voice was calling the unknown helicopter that had just passed over his position. The call sign of the yacht was *Magic*. I circled back and three pairs of eyes strained nearly out of their sockets to see if there was a yacht behind us. The wind had caught us and we were being blown back far too quickly to do a meaningful search. We called the *Magic* on the radio and asked if the helicopter he'd just seen had turned back. He confirmed it had. It must be us. As I retraced our route we simply couldn't find him but I knew he couldn't be far away. I turned back into wind and asked the *Magic* whether he had any flares or smoke left. A few moments later we were rewarded with the sight of a small patch of sea spray turning red – the yacht had to be in the trough beyond. We spotted her. She was in a hell of a state and was taking each wave side-on. Instead of riding smoothly up the wall of water each time, she was being knocked completely flat and then rolling all the way through over 100 degrees until her mast nearly touched the water on the other side. I turned sharply to the right, trying to stay visual with the yacht, then brought the aircraft once again around into wind. The torrential rain was making it almost impossible to see out of the cockpit windscreen and I was having to move my head around a great deal to stay in contact with the boat. As I brought the big Wessex lower and lower the waves grew to mythic proportions.

Two problems: first, there was no way we were going to be able to pick up the crew from the deck of the yacht; the mast and tattered rigging would have swatted Smiler like a fly. Second, the waves were indeed over 40 feet high. Our normal hover height was 15 feet. If I was to have any chance of doing something useful I was going to have to get well down below the crests and ride up each one. There's no way you can lower a man accurately from above 40 feet. There are just not enough visual references and he would have been swinging like a pendulum by the time he hit the water. It was quickly decided between us that Smiler would have to stay attached to the winch wire throughout; if he disengaged himself we might never get him back.

The next task was to brief the crew of the *Magic* on how we were going to try and get them. The only option was to ask them to jump into the water. I don't ever remember hesitating during a rescue before but I did just at that moment. There were five people on the boat beneath me, none of them were injured and they were aboard a boat which, although very battered, was still afloat. I was going to ask them, one by one, to separate themselves from that boat and jump into the water. The moment they did that it would be up to me whether they lived or died. If the aircraft suffered a malfunction or if I'd simply over-estimated my capabilities and found that I couldn't put Smiler into the water accurately enough for him to be able to join hands, then I would have personally signed a man's death warrant.

I asked John and Smiler to wait just a moment while I practised hovering down in the troughs, I had to be at least reasonably certain in my own mind that I was going to be able to hack it. John had abandoned his mapping equipment and taken up station in the open cabin doorway. As I lowered the aircraft down into the waves he kept up his patter of information. I wasn't too bothered about position, the yacht was a couple of hundred yards off to one side of us and it didn't matter if I drifted around a bit to start with. My major concern was to discover if the Wessex would respond quickly enough to ride the waves up and down. I tried experimenting with rhythm. As the crest of a wave passed beneath me I thought about lowering my left hand on the collective lever (height control); this would reduce the power and we'd descend. I watched for the trough and tried to anticipate the moment at which I would then raise the collective lever and start the climb to the crest. Once a couple of waves had passed I was pretty sure I'd got the rhythm sorted out in my head and we began our vertical descent.

We reached the height of 15 feet and things were going pretty well. I was getting into the rhythm and the aircraft was following beautifully. I'd kept my head looking out to the right as not only did this allow me to see through the open door but it also gave me the best chance of gauging my height visually. Then I chanced a look round to the front and nearly had a heart attack. Through the rain-splattered cockpit windscreen the wave in front of us seemed to tower impossibly high and be rushing at us too quickly. I was mesmerised and pulled the lever up a little too quickly. It wasn't any bigger than any of the other waves, I just hadn't ever seen a wave of that size rushing towards me like an express train. I decided to return to looking out of the side.

John called the *Magic* and asked them to prepare their first man. We wanted him with a fully inflated lifejacket and we wanted him to wait until he got a thumbs-up from Smiler before jumping into the water. John made absolutely certain that they understood our instructions – particularly that we only wanted one man in the water at any one time. The last thing I wanted to see was five men in the water; the chances of getting all of them would be too slim.

We hovered over towards the *Magic*, although 'hover' conjures up a rather more stable environment than we were in. Both the yacht and the helicopter were going up 40 feet and then down 40 feet; the trick was to keep the helicopter doing this dance in time with the yacht. We wanted to get fairly close to the *Magic*, first in order to be able to keep each survivor in sight, and secondly so that they didn't have to spend too long in the water between jumping from the yacht and making contact with Smiler. The closer we hovered the easier the flying became as I used the movement of the yacht to give me a visual height reference. We could see the first man gripping a rail on the windward side and struggling to keep his footing. The three of us took a deep breath and I asked, 'Are we ready?'

'Ready, boss,' called John.

'Ready, boss,' called Smiler, with the enthusiasm that went so well with his nickname. He sounded well pumped up.

'OK, give him the thumbs-up.'

Smiler gave the yachtsman the signal while John also called the yacht on the radio. We weren't sure which had the effect but, sure enough, the first man went over the side. With amazing speed the yacht was blown away from him giving us the chance to move in. John raised Smiler on the winch until he was clear of the door and then quickly set him on his way down, calling out my relative position all the time. Although I couldn't see it happening, the stream of information into my earpiece told me that John had dropped Smiler into a nearly perfect position, right next to the survivor. With a practised movement Smiler grabbed the man with one arm while the other moved the double-lift strop around his body, under his arms, and clipped the loose end back on to the winch hook.

He threw both arms out sideways in a thumbs-up gesture and John brought them out of the water together like a cork out of a bottle. The wind set them spinning quite violently, a common problem that was severely disorienting for the diver. All Smiler could do at this point was cling tightly to his man as John brought the winch to a halt just below the aircraft step; if he brought them up too quickly they would break limbs against the aircraft side. He waited a few moments for the spin to die down, then quickly raised the winch, twisted them both around and hauled them on to the cabin decking. Well, that was easier than we thought. We went for it again. One after another we brought four men into the relative safety of the aircraft. They were tired and soaked to the skin but the smiles on their faces were of pure relief.

Smiler himself was beginning to tire. He was expending huge amounts of energy with each lift. We gave him a few moments in the doorway to get his breath back while I hovered away a little in order to relax some muscles. Only one man remained on the *Magic* and I could see that he was not looking forward to the jump into the maelstrom. He was now alone on the boat and was holding on very tightly in the cockpit. Bizarrely he seemed to be wearing glasses and I couldn't imagine how he'd managed to keep them intact against all the violence the sea was throwing at him. Smiler had got his breath back and he indicated to John that he was ready for his last lift. Up went the thumbs and… nothing happened. Our last survivor was either frozen in fear, unable to see us through his salty glasses or not looking the right way. Smiler tried again and again as we willed him to follow his crewmates and jump into the water. Together we were softly calling out to him, as if he could hear us, when suddenly it all came together and he climbed out of the cockpit of the yacht, paused for one short moment, then threw himself into the water – on the *wrong* side.

I guess he must have been manning the radio and hadn't seen the way the others had departed but, whatever the cause, we lost him.

All three of us had shouted 'No' as he went over the leeward side of the boat and, sure enough, the broken yacht just blew right over the top of him. It was leaning over at such an angle that we could see the keel coming up to the surface with each roll, but there was no sign of our man. He had been wearing a lifejacket when we last saw him but the power of the sea must have taken him down beneath the hull and maybe caught him on a part of the ruined rigging that was hanging off the boat in all directions. We desperately looked around for some sign of life. It would be easy to miss him in the churning water if he surfaced away from the boat so our eyes scanned an increasing radius around the abandoned *Magic*. It seemed like a lifetime; it was definitely more than a minute before he suddenly bobbed to the surface at the end of the keel. The boat had driven right over him before releasing him back to the sea and we moved quickly to reclaim him. As he came up on the winch for the last time Smiler had a grin from ear to ear. No longer did I need to stay down in the waves and so, keeping with the rhythm, I pulled in a little extra power and started to climb out of the turmoil. I couldn't begin to move very much until John had them both safely inside but I could afford to relax a little and glance downwards at the winch wire. Not only had our man survived a last look at the underside of his vessel, but he still had his glasses on.

Smiler made our guests as comfortable as possible but the Wessex is little more than a truck in the cabin area and there wasn't much he could do beyond handing out blankets from our stretcher kit. John, meanwhile, had a big task on his hands. We wanted to get our survivors on to terra firma as quickly as we could and I had set off in the approximate direction of Cornwall, but the navigation equipment consisted of little more than a compass. I would have to rely entirely on John's skill in knowing where we'd been and consequently where we now were. We'd been twisting and turning during the search, plus the wind would have been blowing us backwards at an unknown rate

during the hover. One small miscalculation and you could be way off track. We later learned that one of our other aircraft had re-crossed the coast nearly 40 miles out from where he expected to be. It was therefore with no small relief, and frankly my amazement, that John guided us back to the north coastal painters' village of St Ives. We were no more than 100 yards away from the exact point we'd departed land over an hour earlier.

The radio chatter was intense but it seemed that there was more discipline now as each aircraft crew understood more about their own part in the overall picture. It was still only 09.00 in the morning but Dick Harvey's logbook back at Culdrose was filling up rapidly:

0615 Rescue 01 (Nimrod) and Dutch Frigate OVERIJSSEL investigating four men in a liferaft.

0620 Mayday from TARANTULA, no assistance available at this time.

0625 MULLIGATAWNY dismasted, Rescue 97 (Sea King) tasked to assist.

GRIMALKIN capsized 30 miles North West of Lands End, Rescue 21 (Wessex) tasked to assist.

0746 Three survivors sighted in position 50.50N 06.50W. Rescue 21 will transit this position enroute to GRIMALKIN.

0750 Rescue 77 reports he has lifted one casualty from TARANTULA, remainder of Tarantula's crew are remaining onboard.

0755 Further Sea King crew becoming available shortly.

0835 Rescue 20 returning to Culdrose with five survivors from MAGIC, all crewmembers accounted for.

Rescues 77, 79 and 21 all refuelled and returning to the scene of search.

0915 Rescue 97 has picked up two survivors from GRIMALKIN.

0939 Rescue 97 has picked up a further 3 survivors from TROPHY. There are an additional 3, plus one dead, in a liferaft. They have agreed this will be dealt with by the Dutch Frigate.

At 09.50 we landed back at Culdrose. Rescue 97 had beaten us by two minutes with her five survivors and we each had an ambulance to meet us. We'd been airborne for a total of four hours, so we handed our aircraft over to another crew and collared a vehicle to take us to the airfield operations room. Within five minutes our Wessex had been refuelled, taken a good freshwater hosing down the engine intakes and the oncoming crew were ready to go. As we drove off around the perimeter track she overtook us, heading back out into the teeth of the storm.

The radio calls were being written down by our veteran coastguard officer Dick Harvey, while the radar 'plot' was being run by Dave Roue, a great personal friend and a superbly professional observer. (He would later die when his Sea King flew into the water at 120 knots one night.) Dave was one of those who'd responded to the news, found the ops room empty and simply decided to start recording everything he heard on to a map. He had quickly become the prime source of information for all crews, both when returning and prior to launch. Even with the number of aircraft now available it was clear that this was going to be a mammoth job. It wasn't as simple as being tasked, finding your target and picking up the survivors. Along the way you'd spot something in the water, maybe a life raft with men in it or a yacht firing distress flares, and if you didn't record it or deal with it there and then, there was a good chance it would never be seen again. While you were dealing with this new task, somebody else would stumble upon your original target and begin to sort it out and, all the time, aircraft were asking other aircraft for help.

The RAF Nimrod was a great asset. She could move at over 400 knots and therefore quickly take over responsibility for watching over a group in a life raft while the helicopter dealt with another group twenty miles further on. She was also the only aircraft that could simultaneously communicate with all the helicopters hovering down low in the troughs of the waves, and with Culdrose, the coastguards, her own base at St Mawgan and the multiple yachts transmitting their Maydays. It must have been bedlam for her radio operators and in many cases quite painful to listen to the stories unfolding beneath.

We reported all we knew to Dave, whose plot was a patchwork of multi-coloured markings, and headed back to the squadron for a quick bite of breakfast. Or we would have done so if we could have got into the crewroom. The whole squadron was by now streaming in to help and each new arrival was asking what on earth was going on. In the meantime the world's media had been quick off the mark and at least four separate camera crews were filming in a room no bigger than a large domestic sitting room. Household TV names were filing their reports and, of course, a crew returning from 'the front' were fresh meat to talk to. While they were a bit of a shock to us they didn't get in our way at all. There was plenty for them to film and although hard at work themselves they would always stop to hold a door open for the next crew hurtling out. Before long many of them moved off to interview the survivors who, by now, were starting to stretch the capacity of the sick bay.

Our third flight of the day is recorded starkly in my logbook as: 'Fastnet, *Golden Apple*, 4 hours 35 minutes'. At 12.20 John, Smiler and I took over Rescue 21 from the incoming crew who had just picked up all eight yachtsmen from *Camargue*. Our tasking was to join two other helicopters searching for a survivor who'd been seen in the water from the yacht *Festinia Tertia*. This part of the operation is a bit hazy in my memory and even on the day each event had begun to blend seamlessly into the next. The report shows that our mates in Rescue 30 landed Culdrose at 15.23 with a hypothermia case from *Festinia*, so presumably we were successful between us.

The next sequence I remember vividly. We'd been for a fuel top-up on the Scilly Isles and were tasked to pick up the crew of *Golden Apple of the Sun* some 35 miles further out into the Atlantic.

We asked the coastguard how many to expect and were knocked sideways when the answer came back: 'Ten.'

The rain had pretty much stopped around the Scilly Isles and there was even the odd ray of sunshine now and again through the scudding clouds. Even the seas seemed calmer but everything is relative and it was still blowing a force 8 to severe gale 9. *Golden Apple* had lost her rudder completely; this was something that would feature heavily in the post-race analysis by the yachting fraternity as she was one of six yachts carrying new carbon-fibre rudders. We would later learn that this was a 43-foot Irish contender and that her young New Zealand designer Ron Holland was aboard, along with principal helmsman Rodney Pattisson MBE, an Olympic gold and silver medallist in sailing. He was the first Scot ever to win an Olympic medal in sailing and was Great Britain's most successful Olympic sailor right up until 2008.

Even from above, the whole crew looked completely exhausted, albeit clearly a professional team at the very top of the Admiral's Cup rankings. Even without a rudder they had been trying to make it back to safe haven, but forecasts of another big blow that night had persuaded them that discretion was the better part of valour. We established a good radio link and began to consider how to get these ten guys off their disabled boat. Asking them to repeat the process of jumping into the water one by one wasn't appetising. We all felt we'd rolled that dice once too often. Lifting them straight off the deck was again out of the question with the mast swaying drunkenly from side to side.

In the end we settled on a life raft solution. *Golden Apple* had only one inflatable life raft on board. We asked them to inflate it, get into it and let it drift away from the yacht until it was clear enough of the mast for Smiler to descend and pick them up one by one. This would have been a perfect plan if only the life raft would drift away from the yacht, but some peculiar force of nature kept dragging it back alongside. It didn't matter what anybody tried, the thing just kept returning. The only solution we could come up with was to lower Smiler into the water as close as we dared and then let him swim, still attached to our winch line, to the life raft. We hoped we'd then be able to tow Smiler and the life raft far enough away from *Golden Apple* to hover vertically above and pick up the survivors one by one.

This was a lot to ask of Smiler. We'd been up since around 03.00 that morning and it was now getting into late afternoon. He'd already been swimming five times in a force 10 storm with a set of breathing apparatus on his back and we were all starting to feel the cold and the tiredness. But navy divers are cut from a tough cloth and their training includes daily crawls up to their armpits through endless mud flats with the equipment on their back. When you see the Fleet Air Arm crew doing the field gun race at the Royal Tournament, the team is almost always composed of divers.

With the positive and chirpy attitude that we all loved about him, Smiler called 'Ready, boss,' unplugged his intercom and swung out over the water as John and I worked together to drop him as close to the yacht as we could without swatting him with the mast. Once again I had to rely on John's continuous patter on the intercom to guide me.

'He's in the water, I've got a thumbs-up, I'm giving him some slack, he's starting to swim, come up two feet and back two feet, position is good, Smiler's taking a breather, he's setting off again, come forward one, up one, back two, he's got another twenty yards to swim, height's good, position good, ten yards to go, the survivors are trying to paddle towards him, they're leaning over, they've got him, come up two and left two, Smiler's got hold of the dinghy and the survivors have got hold of him, he's taking off his mask, we'll give him a moment to brief them, you're beginning to drift, come back four, he's putting his mask back on, I've got a thumbs-up, we're going to try and tow them, come up two and begin drifting slowly left, that's good, keep coming, keep coming, keep coming, you OK, boss?'

'Yup, how much further?'

'We'll go another twenty feet just to be sure, come down two and keep drifting as you are, fifteen feet, come up one, keep coming, keep coming, ten feet, slow down a little, Smiler is OK but he's struggling to hold on, five feet, two, one, hold your hover, I'm raising Smiler out of the water, he's putting the strop around the first man, come left two, survivor is in the strop, come left another two, you're drifting right, raising the winch, at the door, turning them around, pulling them in, releasing the survivor, strapping him into a seat, he's in the seat, returning to the winch, raising the winch, thumbs-up, lowering the winch, Smiler's going down, come left four feet to re-establish position over the life raft…' and so on, for a total of ten lifts.

The lifting was a relatively straightforward exercise for us so I settled down to learn a poem. This might seem a strange thing to do while flying a rescue chopper but the poem was written on the large flat transom at the stern of the *Golden Apple* and fixating on it was a good technique in maintaining a precise distance from the gradually abandoned yacht.

Every so often, without moving my head, my eyes would glance inside the cockpit at the fuel and the engine instruments. Fuel was fine, although we'd need to take more from the Scilly Isles before returning home, but the engines were starting to clog. The constant sea spray borne on the gale was being sucked down the intakes and the salt coating was clearly growing. We were using a fairly constant power setting but the intake temperature was slowly rising. We'd seen this happening all day and it wasn't yet cause for alarm but it did need monitoring.

By the time the last of the ten-man crew was safely on his way up to the cabin door I was word-perfect on the poem.

Though I am old with wandering
Through hollow lands and hilly lands
I will find out where she has gone

And kiss her lips and take her hands
And walk among long dappled grass
And pluck till time and times are gone
The silver apples of the moon
The golden apples of the sun

We all exhaled loudly as the last man took the last spot on the cabin floor and I'd never been so glad to hear Smiler plug back into the intercom.

'Nice one, boss.'

'You OK?'

'Bit tired, can we go home now?'

'On our way.'

A quick suck of fuel on the Scillies and we really were on our way. Just another forty minutes and we'd be back at base.

At 16.55 our wheels touched down for the last time that day and our ten passengers were helped to the waiting ambulances. We'd been on the go for a good fourteen hours and spent more than eight and a half of them airborne, but it was nothing compared to what the yachtsmen had been through. Never the less it was time for John, Smiler and me to hand over to a fresher crew, get some food, get some sleep and be back for the following dawn. Our squadron total for that day would be 29 hours 35 minutes of flying by nightfall, using only four helicopters. The longer-range Sea Kings could fly on into the night and would end up with a total of 49 hours by midnight, using five airframes.

Fastnet '79 is the largest and most effective maritime rescue operation ever mounted in peacetime in the UK. I'm proud to have been a part of it and proud to have been the first helicopter airborne on the first morning. But in an age of GPS, instantaneous mapping systems, infrared thermal search cameras and automated tracking devices, it's hard to convey the sheer scale of the chaos of this event.

The second and third days of rescue operations were a mopping-up exercise. Abandoned yachts were checked, deflated life rafts were pulled from the sea and exhausted yacht crews were monitored as they made their way back to safe haven, but no additional lives were saved.

I don't remember any point at which it felt as though we, or any of the other crews, had made a bad decision, but who can ever possibly know? I do know that as aviators we deal in a lot of 'what-if?' scenarios. What if an engine fails, what will be my actions? What if my fuel state gets to the point where I can only go to Ireland, not back to Cornwall? One particular question haunted me: What if I see a flare when I'm en route to another assigned target? I never properly resolved all the combinations of possibilities. Thankfully my own crew were never put to the test with a conflict of interest but these things lurked in the back of my mind throughout the task on day one. We were all in the same frame of mind. Get out there as fast as possible, pluck as many people from the water as possible, and get them back on to dry land.

I recently read the extraordinary book *Left For Dead* by Nick Ward, the last man to be picked up alive after having been left in the cockpit of *Grimalkin* with a dead compatriot for most of the night of the thirteenth and all day of the fourteenth. According to his introduction, it took Nick thirty years to get to the point where he could write the story. Having witnessed at first hand the seas he writes about, I couldn't put the book down until I'd finished it. I went back to my own records of that day and found the notes of Dick Harvey, our coastguard liaison officer, who so diligently tried to keep track of events alongside Dave Roue in the operations room at Culdrose: assimilate the information, put it on a map, retask the airborne crews, disseminate the information, do it all again. I've already listed some of the entries from Dick's log but I repeat the remainder of his notes from just that first day below, in the hope

that it conveys some sense of the sheer scale of the task and the extraordinary lengths that everybody went to in sorting logic and fact out of chaos and confusion. (SK = Sea King, WX = Wessex.)

R97 (SK) landed on Culdrose 0946Z with five survivors who were admitted to Culdrose Sick Bay, and at 0948Z R20 (WX) landed on, her five survivors were also admitted to Sick Bay.

From R21 (WX) at 1020Z returning with 8 survivors from CAMARGUE: All yacht's crew accounted for.

R98 (SK) reports returning Culdrose at 1037Z with one survivor on board in a bad way, picked up in position 50.54N 07.25W. R98 (SK) instructed to proceed direct to Treliske Hospital Truro.

Backup Sea King 304 arriving from Prestwick ETA 1220Z.

1137Z R97 (SK) tasked with R20 (WX) to make pick up in position 50.45N 06.42W where five persons reported in a dinghy. R20 (WX) Double lifted five survivors at 1155Z from SKIDBLADNER in position 50.46N 06.42W returning to Culdrose.

R97 (SK) reports proceeding to one person in the water in position 50.55N 07.50W.

R98 (SK) returned Culdrose from Treliske, landed on 1200Z.

Report from R77 (SK) double lifted twelve survivors at 1213Z. Six from GAN in position 50.41N 07.38W and six from HELSTRUL in position 50.43N 07.35W. R77 (SK) landed on 1217Z survivors admitted to Culdrose Sick Bay, aircraft refuelled. At 1225Z R20 (WX) returned with her survivors and refuelled.

R98 (SK) returned to scene of search 1225Z.

R77 (SK) and R30 (WX) returned search area 1250Z, and R25 (WX) at 1310Z.

1301Z From Lands End MRSC. Report received from Bishops Rock Lighthouse. Yacht observed 5 miles SSW of rock, no longer visible, request helo investigates.

R97 (SK) have double lifted seven survivors from GRINGO in position 50.56N 07.30W, one of the survivors has a broken rib. GRINGO's crew all accounted for. Only 30 minutes endurance left, returning Culdrose.

1407Z R97 (SK) and R20 (WX) land on to refuel. Two Lynx helicopters from Yeovilton to assist.

1439Z R96 (SK) returned to scene of search, and R463 (LYNX) at 1515Z.

1502Z From R25 (WX) returning to Culdrose to refuel, landed on 1507Z.

R77 (SK) and R21 (WX) airborne to position 295 Round Island 30 miles, to search for survivor in the water, believed to be from FESTINIA.

1512Z R30 (WX) reports returning with hypothermia case from FESTINIA. Landed on 1523Z.

R21 (WX) tasked to position 50.16N 07.18W to pick up ten crew members from GOLDEN APPLE.

R25 (WX) airborne and tasked to work with R77 (SK) 1529Z.

R90 (SK) tasked by SRCC at 1550Z to search area on the south and west of Scillies.

R98 (SK) returning to Culdrose with two survivors on board, one from GUNSLINGER in position 51.23N 07.22W and one from FLASHLIGHT in position 50.23N 07.07W at 1618Z, ETA 7/8 minutes. Landed Culdrose 1628Z. Casualties admitted to Sick Bay.

From R21 (WX) returning with ten survivors, complete crew of GOLDEN APPLE in position 50.16N 07.18W. ETA 55 minutes.

R25 (WX) have double lifted four survivors at 1647Z from FLASHLIGHT in position 50.23N 07.03W. All crew of FLASHLIGHT now accounted for.

R77 (SK) returning Culdrose 1716Z, no survivors on board. Land on 1735Z.

R21 (WX) returning scene of search at 1722Z, tasked to work with Nimrod, search area 50.20N 06.20W – 51.00N 07.30W.

1735Z Warship BROADSWORD to assume duties as CSS.

1630Z R463 (LYNX) returned Culdrose to refuel.

R96 (SK) returning Culdrose with eleven survivors on board 1755Z. Five from ALLAMANDA in position 50.30N 07.30W and six from BILLY BONES in position 50.40N 07.30W. Crews of both yachts accounted for.

WEATHER IN THE SEARCH AREA SOUTHWESTERLY GALE 8 TO SEVERE GALE 9, SHOWERS, GOOD VISIBILITY.

1755Z From SRCC via R90 (SK) 7/8 yachts in difficulties in position 50.40N 07.40W. Warship BROADSWORD's position 7 miles NW Scillies, searching the area.

R96 (SK) landed on, survivors admitted to Sick Bay. R96 (SK) returned scene of search 1842Z. R463 (LYNX) to scene of search 1915Z.

R21 (WX) returning one survivor and one body on board 1925Z from GRIMALKIN.

1930Z R747 (LYNX) to scene of search.

1930Z R90 (SK) returned to refuel and rejoined search at 1955Z. Sitrep at 1955Z.

R96 (SK) tasked to work with Dutch Frigate OVERIJSSEL.

R463 (LYNX) tasked to position 50.17N 07.15W to investigate life rafts, yachts and life-jackets.

1957Z R25 (WX) reports the following yachts sighted in positions:- FLASHLIGHT 50.20N 07.10W. Helm secured, sea anchor streamed, Abandoned.

GOLDEN PRINCESS 50.18N 07.08W. OK.

GOLDEN APPLE OF THE SUN 50.19N 07.15W Abandoned.

R25 (WX) returning to base.

2030Z R20 (WX) sighted 17 yachts, visibility too bad to continue.

2035Z R463 (LYNX) and R747 (LYNX) returning Culdrose.

2230Z R96 (SK) returned Culdrose.
0030Z R90 (SK) returned to Culdrose.
AIRFIELD NOW CLOSED UNTIL FIRST LIGHT. SEA
KINGS PLACED AT 15 MINUTES NOTICE.

It's a truism in the Navy that however serious anything has become there will always be a moment of light relief. And the more serious the circumstances perhaps the greater the release that humour provides. Sure enough, on the fourth day, two Germans appeared in the crewroom just before breakfast time. They came from *Stern*, a glossy German news magazine that specialised in great pictures and minimal text. Their story of finding us was something of a survival story of its own. In halting English it seemed to consist of cancelled airliner flights, sunken ferry boats, broken charter planes, incompetent taxi drivers and on through a plethora of mishaps which had led to them spending three full days and nights on the road towards capturing one of the biggest news stories of the year. By the time they had reached our crewroom they were exhausted themselves.

All the other news crews had gone home by now and the morning was turning into a bright summer's day. It was the turn of Jamie Bauld to fry the breakfast. He was the archetypical Scotsman, so broad in his language that no Englishman, let alone a German, could fully understand everything he said, and exhibiting the sort of tight-fisted approach for which the Scots are famed. In fact, he revelled in it and turned it into an art form. Never the less he took pity on the Germans and included them in the breakfast arrangements. Jamie duly produced a classic SAR fry-up with all the works, which our new friends wolfed down with enthusiasm. At the end of the meal as Jamie was doing the washing-up, the reporter sidled up to him and pressed two crisp fifty-pound notes into his hand, muttering something about a contribution to the coffee fund.

'Good grief, man,' exclaimed Jamie. 'If I'd known you were going to do that, I'd have given you two eggs.' I defy anyone to find a tougher, more professional or funnier bunch of guys than I had the privilege to serve with on the Fastnet, or any of our other rescue escapades.

Survivors and bodies picked up by helicopter, in chronological order.

Day One – 13 August

TARANTULA	1		Sea King
MAGIC	5	Complete crew	**My Team**
GRIMALKIN	2		Sea King
TROPHY	3		Sea King
CAMARGUE	8	Complete crew	Wessex
ARIADNE	1		Sea King
SKIDBLADNER	5		Wessex
GAN	6		Sea King
HELSTRUL	6		Sea King
GRINGO	7	Complete crew	Sea King
FESTINIA TERTIA	1		Wessex
GUNSLINGER	1		Sea King
FLASHLIGHT	1		Sea King
GOLDEN APPLE	10	Complete crew	**My Team**
FLASHLIGHT	4	Crew now complete	Wessex
ALLAMANDA	5		Sea King
BILLY BONES	6		Sea King
GRIMALKIN	2	One dead	Wessex

Day Two – 14 August
None

Day Three – 15 August

HELSTRUL   1   Dead   Sea King

Day Four – 16 August

BON ADVENTURE   1   Broken arm   Sea King

Statistics

Yachts started	303
Yachts finished	85
Yachts retired	189
Yachts abandoned	24
Yachts lost believed sunk	5
Lives saved	136
Lives lost	15

FASTNET REVISITED

RECENTLY I HAPPENED TO STUMBLE upon a news item about a memorial that had been dedicated at the twenty-fifth anniversary of the Fastnet event in 2004. A ceremony had been held at the Cape Clear Island Museum and Archive, just four miles away from the Fastnet Rock in County Cork, Ireland, at which the names of the deceased were read out as wreaths were cast on the waters. Over 400 people attended, Ted Turner donated a painting of his yacht *Tenacious* winning the '79 event, and two of the crew who had survived the disaster established the 'Fastnet Race Remembrance Collection'. By an extraordinary coincidence, they were both members of *Magic* and *Golden Apple* crews, which my own team had rescued.

Not really expecting an answer, I sent an email off to the originator of the project and the website, Dr Eamon Lankford. Within 24 hours he had not only replied but had put me in touch with the two crew members, Peter Whipp (skipper of *Magic*) and

Neil Kenefick (trimmer and offshore driver of *Golden Apple*), giving me the opportunity to ask them about their perspective of the brief moment our lives had come together.

Peter Whipp, of *Magic*, responded:

We were one of the earlier boats to get into trouble; the rudder snapped clean away at about half past midnight. We were lucky because I sensed trouble in the previous afternoon on seeing a huge halo around the sun. It was quite uncanny and I saw that all our loose things were lashed down and used a little portable generator which we had to charge up our battery; we had no engine on Magic. *We were probably the smallest boat in the fleet and I believe that we were doing quite well in the race.*

The charged battery gave us VHF right up to the time you pulled us out which enabled us to know what was going on and to relay messages back to the rescue team. Just before you arrived, we saw a Nimrod and we spoke to the pilot and he verified that it was us who was speaking to him by banking left and then right. We told him that we were in no immediate danger and settled in to wait for the storm to abate. We were OK but with two crew members suffering from panic.

I remember when you came by I protested that we would be OK but you had more sense and told us that it would be a waste if you returned empty just to get some more fuel. That sealed it. Our crew was myself and four others. I think one of the stronger two went first to show the nervous two the way. As tradition dictates, I came last. I can't remember getting off the wrong side but the boat did spin around regularly. I swam away from the boat and your diver came down for me. Then something went wrong, I only had one arm in the loop and the diver didn't have a proper hold of me and so he let me back into the water. You explained back in Culdrose that you had to fly around a little to regain

your concentration which, of course, I fully understand, but the memory of seeing you fly away without me and my boat a few very big waves upwind of me will remain with me forever.

I then remember getting into the helicopter to find that it was full of water and so the diver and, I think, your navigator tried to push it out of the door with his flippers. I wanted to be back on my boat despite the fact that we knew that she had sustained some structural damage; she was built of wood.

I have never wanted to read any of the books about the race although I did help a Canadian journalist write one because we met up with a Canadian boat called Evergreen as she was making her way back to Cornwall and we met up with their crew again after the race in Plymouth.

I can never thank you enough for rescuing us. It was an experience I never want to repeat but I did force myself back on to the sea and I do still sail. I went back to do the Fastnet Race in 1981, 1983 and then won it overall in 1985.

I was thrilled to get this response and amazed at Peter's two recollections. First, I had no memory at all of talking him into being airlifted but I do remember a certain fear associated with what might happen if we left a yacht that had been so hard to find.

John Charnley, my crewman, was constantly dividing his time between being an essential pair of eyes and a 'dead reckoning' navigator, scribbling times, tracks and positions on to a paper map with a pencil. Remember there was no GPS, no sophisticated moving maps; we could only have knowledge of our position by virtue of passing over a known point such as a lighthouse. To that we could sometimes add a radio bearing that told us we were in such and such a direction from RAF St Mawgan, but usually we were at such low level that they were of no use to us.

All the while we would be straining to assimilate aural information from several radio sources and from each other. This formed into a 3D virtual world in our heads and through years of practice it was a surprisingly accurate world, but the moment you returned to base for fuel or to drop off survivors you would have to 'reboot' the 3D world in your head and start again as circumstances had changed so much in the short time you were off-task. Perhaps that was partly why we were reluctant to leave Peter and his crew aboard *Magic*.

Peter's second comment about the effect it had on him of me 'flying away' was sobering indeed. He's referring to how difficult it was for Smiler to catch him in the waves and how we had therefore backed off to start a fresh run at collecting Peter. To us it was all part of the normal routine. After several unsuccessful attempts at threading a needle in bad light we all know how a pause, a deep breath and a fresh start will often yield a perfect conclusion right at the start of the second attempt. That's how it was for us that day as we hovered sideways: it gave Smiler a chance to catch his breath in the water and me a chance to flex my finger muscles. We probably moved no further than 30 metres away from Peter's position and took no longer than 30 seconds to reconvene for the fresh attempt, but to Peter we were no longer directly over his head and were probably hidden behind each wave as it came tumbling through our field of play. To him it was as if we had flown away and left him.

From Neil Kenefick of *Golden Apple* I also received an interesting fresh perspective but one that matched my own memory:

We had one life raft manufactured in the USA, very lightweight!! I recall sending out the Pan Pan. Suddenly you were there. We put Rodney Pattisson (MBE) on the radio. We then launched the raft and the rope broke, Rodney dived into the raft and I threw a rope to him. The raft was very shoddy. We then boarded and we were underwater with 10 aboard, with the roof collapsed. The raft would not separate from Golden Apple. *I recall looking up at you in the sky and throwing her on her side to get the down draft to blow* Golden Apple *away so you could then hover and take us 1 by 1.*

Neil also forwarded my email to Ron Holland, the designer of *Golden Apple*, who also kindly replied:

Neil sent me your chapter and preceding communication. I think you can understand reading this brought back memories. (Like when I read Left For Dead*).*

My recollections:

– Aware of good communications with the heli.

– Feeling guilty about leaving a mostly good yacht. After hearing the weather was to deteriorate again, evening coming on and with the Scillies to leeward, we all agreed to go.

– Inflating a raft (we only had one raft) in 40+ knots of wind on the deck of a small yacht was a challenge. (The height of the storm was over.) The umbilical cord tore away from the raft and we kept it close to the leeward side with difficulty.

– The raft did not fully inflate and I felt very claustrophobic jammed chest deep in water with my crew mates.

– The raft was pinned under the lee side of Golden Apple *of the Sun, drifting quickly downwind on top of the raft.*

– We had the impression the heli downdraft helped separate the yacht from the raft?

– Hugh Coveney, the owner and I, were the last two to be saved. Before he left me in the arms of the wireman: 'For God's sake, Holland, who would have thought it would end like this?'

– In the chopper we first learnt of the devastation the Fastnet Race fleet had experienced. That was shocking.

The final postscript must come from one of the smallest boats in the fleet which survived the storm and crept into Plymouth late on Friday 17 August, having sat out a second storm on the Thursday night. The skipper signed his declaration: 'Retired due to inclement weather.'

CIVVY STREET

ALL GOOD THINGS MUST COME TO AN END. When I'd first donned a uniform in 1972, the prospect of eight years in a blue suit seemed to stretch into infinity but as the aftermath of Fastnet continued into the end of 1979 I began to realise that next year would be my last in the Fleet Air Arm. I say 'aftermath' because the event had not only attracted huge attention at the time of the stricken race but also continued to do so for the months that followed as various organisations questioned their rules, their structure and their roles. The Royal Yachting Association and the Royal Ocean Racing Association set about generating the official report and enquiry, which was eagerly awaited by the yachting fraternity around the world. Yacht design had been changing rapidly as technologies developed and components made from new materials such as carbon fibre were introduced. Questions had to be asked about whether some of the ancient wisdom of vessel design had been forgotten in the headlong rush towards speed at all cost.

At the same time there was immense public interest in the multitude of personal stories of bravery, tragedy and human strength in the face of adversity. Although our little crewroom was no longer bursting at the seams with television cameras and our routine had returned to relative normality, there was still a steady stream of reporters from both national and international publications interviewing the duty crew in an attempt to cement all the final pieces of the jigsaw into place.

Our regular presentations to local organisations had become particularly popular and there's no doubt that the attention of these audiences had significantly increased, along with their sizes. We also ventured much further afield in order to say thank you to those who had played their own part in providing manpower, skills or hardware. The CO tried to divide up the responsibilities fairly among us, woven in between the day-to-day SAR operations that inexorably continued. My own highlight was a flight to Farnsworth, near Manchester, to visit the Rolls Royce factory where our engines had been assembled. It was a rare opportunity to fly outside the usual confines of our patch and entailed the study of air-traffic structures in regions that were unfamiliar to us in order to arrive safely at the appointed hour. We landed in the car park and were ushered on to the podium in a cavernous workspace full of over 1,500 enthusiastic individuals who were keen to hear stories of how their product had helped to save lives.

The Royal Western Yacht Club, being the hosts at the finish line of the Fastnet race, were also generous in inviting all of our aircrew to a black tie prize-giving dinner in late November. It was inevitably an event tinged with sadness and introspection for those for whom the race had been their last but we were honoured to be a part of it. The invitation letter had specifically said that the vice commodore would do no more than simply welcome us as guests. Thus we were able to relax and enjoy the company of our hosts in the unfamiliar civilian environment.

Three months later an unexpected letter arrived from FONAC, the admiral in command of the Fleet Air Arm:

3 March 1980

Dear Grayson

I am delighted to inform you that Her Majesty the Queen has approved the award of Her Commendation for Valuable Service in the Air to you in recognition of your outstanding contribution to the rescue of participants in last year's Fastnet Race. Please accept my heartiest congratulations.

Until the publication of the award in the *London Gazette* on 4 March you should keep this news to your immediate family. You will be informed of the arrangements for the presentation of your award in due course.

Your sincerely
Rear Admiral Edward Anson
Flag Officer Naval Air Command

At the subsequent ceremony my crew, Albie's crew and two of the Culdrose Sea King crews were formally presented with the oak leaves to be worn on the chest of our uniform.

By that time I was studying hard. I was still only 24 but the date of my discharge was rapidly approaching and I needed the licence that would allow me to fly as a civilian. The Navy was very aware of its responsibilities and gave every leaver the opportunity to study for and apply for a new career. The correspondence course for the Airline Transport Pilot's Licence (ATPL) was just about the hardest studying I ever had to undertake. Initial flying training for the Navy had been an ordeal but at least I was doing it in the company of others. Burning the midnight oil alone took some getting used to.

Bizarrely the Civil Aviation Authority made very little distinction between the exam requirements for a commercial helicopter pilot and those required to qualify as an airline captain. Learning about navigation equipment that is only used when flying trans-oceanic seemed like a pointless exercise when your fuel was unlikely to last beyond the furthermost lighthouse, but there was no argument to be had so I just knuckled down to it. By June of 1980 the hard work had paid off and I was the proud holder of an ATPL (Helicopters).

It was all very well working towards a licence but the landscape of opportunity was then almost too wide. The extra gratuity to stay in the Navy and the addition of a pension (at 29) was certainly tempting, but deep down inside I knew that if I took the easy route it would be something I'd regret. It would be back to sea and another four years of 'Yes, sir, no, sir'. So I firmly resolved to take the eight-year break point that I'd been working towards.

At that time the accepted career path was to apply for a job on the North Sea. The oil industry was booming and most of my contemporaries had found that the jobs on offer were well paid and not dissimilar to the Navy life to which they had become accustomed. The cold and wet climate around Aberdeen didn't seem to bother them and the long and dull hours carrying a helicopter full of oil-rig workers across a grey ocean to a huge structure looming out of the fog seemed to suit those who had stayed operational on Sea Kings. The Sikorsky S61 was simply a stretched civilian version of the Sea King, so that brought another familiar aspect to the job, but the idea of piloting an airframe I had been used to in a military context as a kind of a taxi didn't sit well with me.

Quite out of the blue I got it into my head that I would like to start a helicopter company. I don't have any recollection of arriving at that decision by a logical path, it was just suddenly there as an absolute certainty in the forefront of my plans. In many ways it was an unrealistic aspiration; I had no business training whatsoever and the price of a good second-hand helicopter was many hundreds of thousands of pounds. I also arrived at the arrogant and self-limiting decision that I was going to do this in the county of Cornwall and in collaboration with an old friend, Keith Thompson. Keith and I had shared a cabin on the *Ark* and he was due to come out of the Navy just a couple of months before me. He was still away at sea at the time so I pressed on in the assumption that he'd be up for this new adventure.

Very short letters of proposal were despatched to just about every successful company in the south-west, and very short letters of rejection soon came flooding back. However, the letter I composed to a local car dealer was written rather more carefully. Rumour had it that he owned the only private helicopter in the county and that he had achieved local notoriety by buying it in order to get round the loss of his driving licence for speeding. The response came by phone the next day and Keith (recently returned from sea) and I were soon on the way to Liskeard, at the other end of the county from Culdrose, to meet the famed Mr Roy Flood. The helicopter, which he kept in a neat hangar next to his country home, was beautiful. Having spent the best part of my career to date in the Wessex, this Longranger seemed to be little more than a flimsy toy. It was immaculately kept, had smooth leather seats and there was not a drop of oil to be seen on the aircraft or the hangar floor. This was all new to me.

Before the day was over we'd sketched out a plan. Following on from my proposal we agreed that Roy would continue to use G-LRII for his private pursuits but that Keith and I would form a company with him to operate it on commercial activities. We went on to talk about how we might structure the arrangement and about how it might be better to build another hangar next to Castle Motors, Roy's company which would fund the start-up. Roy had also phoned his flying instructor to book me in for a conversion course and I began to grasp the first understanding of how some parts of the commercial world didn't hold committee meetings and insist on piles of paperwork. This would be the style of operation for the next ten years in what was immediately named Castle Air Charters.

There were still some months to go before my official naval flying duties would come to an end. Commercial charters and company preparations had therefore to be squeezed in between my regular SAR duties. I completed the flying conversion course to the new Longranger and began to make a few trips around the country with Roy as he went from auction to auction in the pursuit of good value cars to sell from his forecourt. On SAR duty days I no longer had the luxury of watching television in the squadron crewroom as there were operations manuals to be written and all the paraphernalia of a new company to be sorted out. I now had a desk of my own in Liskeard and the ninety-minute drive from one job to the other was made at every spare opportunity. By June of 1980 we had gained the licence from the Civil Aviation Authority to begin commercial operations, and Keith and I alternated our time between the Navy and Castle Air. We began to fly short pleasure trips at various events around the country, an activity that didn't stretch the aviator in me but opened my eyes to the connection between flying hours, company income and an eventual salary.

On 2 July a small conflict arose in the calendar. I had the morning SAR duty but also a commitment at Castle Air to fly some Euro MPs on a tour around Cornwall, beginning from Falmouth. The timings would work out OK if I took the Longranger home with me, finished SAR at the usual time of midday, then jumped into my civilian role to fly off to Falmouth. But a helicopter isn't something you can just park in the driveway of a semi-detached house in a small town. The only option was to ask the CO if he minded me keeping the Longranger on the squadron apron overnight, prior to the afternoon flight to Falmouth. Permission was sought from the captain of the airbase and happily given. I positioned up from Liskeard to Culdrose late on the evening of the first, came into work at dawn on the second, flew a couple of sorties and then gave the boys a few minutes of prodding my strange but beautiful new toy before climbing out of one uniform and into another, leaving the afternoon SAR crew to take over my Wessex. The juxtaposition of one career with another and the almost seamless transition between the two felt strange but exciting.

On 2 September 1980 I flew my last flight in a Wessex. It was an unremarkable flight that went down in the logbook as 'Coastal patrol'. In fact, it was a flight of pure self-indulgence, visiting all the places around the coast of Cornwall that had played such a big part in my formative years. We went and bounced our wheels on the Camel's Head for the last time, took some pictures and generally enjoyed the last hour in the flying machine that had shared so much of the drama. The next day I packed up my small locker, shook hands and exchanged insults with the boys and drove across the airfield to return my flying helmet.

There was to be one last typical naval moment when I went for my leaving medical. The procedure is more intense than the joining examination: designed to ensure that you can't come back in a few years' time and claim that the Navy caused your bad back or your pathological aversion to bacon rolls. My old friend Rick Jolly, a fantastic surgeon commander who later ran the field hospital in San Carlos Bay in the Falklands (see his book *The Red and Green Life Machine*), conducted the examination. We went through all the usual rituals including stripping down to briefs and performing various balancing and coordination tasks. Knowing that this would be a more strenuous medical than usual I complied without question when Rick told me to take off my Y fronts, put both hands out in front of me, close my eyes, stand on one leg and balance there for as long as possible. I was just priding myself on my ability to remain in that position when he told me to relax and open my eyes. There before me stood a very cute nurse holding up a score-card while Rick doubled over with tears of mirth running down his face. I was going to miss much of the fun and irreverence of Navy life.

But my involvement with the Navy didn't entirely end at that point. There would be one last involvement in an SAR story from a civilian perspective, which I will tell later.

During our first year at Castle Air it became clear that the commercial operation was hindering Roy's ability to fly around the country purchasing cars, so the Castle Motors cash-flow funded the purchase of a second helicopter: a brand new Jetranger. The British pound bought a lot of dollars back in 1981 so it was only a few months later that a third helicopter joined the stable.

At Castle Air the assumption was that if you needed something doing, you did it yourself. We needed a bigger hangar so we just built one. I learned how to drive a JCB backhoe to prepare the ground, we laid concrete during the day, then polished it all night until you could play billiards on the surface. Massive trucks turned up with long and heavy RSJs but it wasn't in Roy's nature to buy pre-prepared steel so I learned to cut with oxy-acetylene and to join by arc-welding. It was a jigsaw puzzle where you had to make all the pieces yourself and then put them together with a crane.

On New Year's Day 1982 (no days off when there's business to be done). I was way up at the top of a scaffolding tower carefully welding together two extremely large RSJs when somebody shouted from ground level that my wife was on the phone.

'Tell her I'll call her back later,' I hollered to the floor below.

'No, she says you'll want to hear this and you have to come now.'

I clambered my way down the four flights of wooden ladder we'd lashed together, in direct opposition to any concept of health and safety, and took the phone.

'Are you sitting down?' my wife asked.

'No, I'm standing holding a telephone cord through the office window with a welding mask on my head.'

'I think you should sit down.'

'Look, I'm really busy at the moment,' I grumbled. 'Why are you calling me at work?'

'You're in the New Year's Honours List. You've been awarded the Air Force Cross.'

I sat down.

To this day I have no idea how this happened, who submitted the recommendation nor who judged it but, sure enough, I was named in both the local and national papers that were lying around in the showroom as being the only recipient of the Air Force Cross that year. Suddenly I had letters after my name. I climbed back up the scaffolding, picked up the welding torch and welded 'Jerry AFC' in very big letters to the side of the RSJ.

Apparently you would normally know of the award in advance, as indicated by the letter post-marked Buckingham Palace that eventually turned up saying, 'Please keep this to yourself and your immediate family until…' It also contained advice that 'the investiture by Her Majesty the Queen will take place at Buckingham Palace on a date to be advised'.

It was long before the days of Google and our little library in Liskeard didn't have the sort of reference section I needed in order to discover exactly what it was that I'd been awarded, so I took myself off to the big county library in the seafaring city of Plymouth to work it out.

Instituted in 1918, the Air Force Cross (AFC) was issued for acts of gallantry while flying on non-active operations to warrant officers and officers of the Royal Air Force. It was later made available to equivalent ranks in the Royal Navy and Army for acts of gallantry in the air.

Simply put, it was the highest gallantry award for flying that could be awarded in peace time. I was totally bowled over.

Over the course of time more letters followed from the palace to secure the arrangement. I dug out my uniform, my wife and mother bought new hats, and off we went to see the Queen. Dad had died a couple of years earlier and had left me the considerable sum (for the time) of £6,000. In his last two years he had risen to become the managing director of Ferrari in the UK so, in his honour and memory, I had blown the whole lot on a Ferrari 308 with the appropriate number 'RU 27' (my age that year). Thus came the spring morning when I drove my Ferrari through the gates of Buckingham Palace and parked it in the central courtyard.

The day passed in a blur. A lady who bore more than a passing resemblance to Queen Elizabeth II shook my hand, said a few kind words and handed me a box containing an unfeasibly large silver cross. By six o'clock I was being interviewed in the studios of the BBC National News programme *Nationwide*, which had run a documentary series two years earlier about our day-to-day life on 771 squadron. I have no idea what I said nor where we went to celebrate, but it was still a day to remember for ever.

In due course the bigger twin-engined Agusta 109 was added to the fleet at Castle Air and about that time a rather grey man in an equally grey suit arrived at our offices in a grey Ford, unannounced. Our initial impression was entirely unfair and he turned out over the course of around three years to be an interesting guy with an interesting job. He came from the Admiralty Underwater Weapons Establishment (AUWE) and his job was to test new torpedoes. His problem lay in the fact that he needed a rather large swathe of sea-space in which to set these monsters running and that space had of course to be entirely clear of civilian boats before he could start the day's work. Despite promulgating the activities, the odd

sailor inevitably failed to read the warnings and strays like this were frequently bringing his tests to a premature halt. He needed a helicopter with a loudspeaker attached that could patrol the weapons range and shout at errant yachtsmen who looked like they were about to wander into danger.

We fitted a loudspeaker arrangement into the side of one of our Jetrangers and began the task. It was an extremely good commercial activity for us and not a particularly demanding job for the pilot. We knew the protocols to adopt when talking to submariners on the radio and the task of patrolling the ocean was entirely familiar. For the AUWE, who could never get hold of a Navy helicopter on the days they needed one, our relative cost was as nothing when compared to the savings they were making in trial days that would otherwise have been lost.

In most cases the yachties would take our 'advice' in good grace, give us a cheery wave and reverse their direction. We only once lost a couple of hours to a small green sailing boat that simply refused to deviate from the course he was on. My calls to him over the loudspeaker were entirely ignored, to the extent that I began to wonder if he was deaf. But he couldn't be blind as well, as he proved when I hovered in front of him and he obliged me with the internationally recognized maritime signal of raising his middle finger. The submarine was loitering in the area at periscope depth but for some reason I couldn't raise him on the radio and I could see from the periscope wake that he was in a turn that would bring him right underneath the sailing boat.

The level of my voice over the loudspeaker went up a couple of octaves as I shouted, 'There is a submarine behind you. If you do not alter ninety degrees to starboard NOW you are in SERIOUS danger.' The bearded yachtie glanced casually over his shoulder but was suddenly galvanised into action and threw his tiller hard to starboard. The submarine was completely unaware of the yacht and from the direction that its periscope was looking it seemed to me that he was studying something on the shore to the north. I descended to the hover in front of the periscope lens and frantically waved and pointed in the direction of the yacht. The periscope whipped around and almost appeared to bulge like a cartoon eye. Only seconds later I could see the huge black shadow roll quite violently as the captain must have shouted, 'Hard to port'. I could only imagine the sound of breaking tea cups in the tin tube as submariners scrabbled for support. From my lofty point of view I could see the prominent sonar bulge at the very bows of the submarine pass less than 10 feet behind the yacht as the sub went one way and the yacht went the other. One very lucky sailor lived to sail another day.

Once we were entirely sure that the weapons range was clear, we would authorise the warship or submarine to carry out a live run and release the torpedo. The 'fish' would do its thing and, at the end of its run, it would inflate a little lifejacket collar and pop to the surface for recovery. At this point a small fishing-boat-like vessel would take our guidance to the floating torpedo and begin the process of trying to recover it using their on-board crane.

The process of recovery took a long time and the light was often fading too quickly to allow us to carry out a second firing, so I asked why they had never attempted torpedo recovery using a helicopter. It had apparently been tried in the past but the recovery contraption beneath the helicopter was over-complicated and failed more often than not. I was intrigued by this problem and that night I retired to the bathroom with a half-used can of hairspray (it floated nicely in the vertical position of an expended torpedo), a small fishing net, some lengths of string and some bent paperclips. By the time I'd finished my hands were wrinkly but I had successfully and repeatedly recovered my 'torpedo'. The recovery net looked like an inverted shuttlecock and was suspended from the helicopter by two ropes. When the release button for the cargo hook was pressed, the relative lengths of the two ropes changed and thus closed the bottom of the net, allowing the helicopter to smoothly lift the torpedo out of the water in the upright position.

Over the coming months my bathroom experimentation was actioned, the real-sized thing was manufactured by AUWE, and we went on to use it successfully. It was a classic win/win whereby we were able to use the more expensive Agusta 109 – the Jetranger and Longranger helicopters didn't have the external lifting capacity for a torpedo – and would often be asked to position to other weapon ranges as far north as the Isle of Skye. The AUWE, meanwhile, achieved many more trial runs each day and thus saved hundreds of thousands of pounds in manpower and vessels. I later learned that every warship in the Royal Navy had been issued with one of my nets but it was a long time before I understood the concept of intellectual property rights so I have nothing to show for it beyond great pride.

It was good still to have a naval connection but the 109 was not really designed for long periods of hovering and lifting. The sleek helicopter was better suited to the fast cruise. Over time the torpedo recovery task took its toll on our helicopters and, as I was to find out later, very nearly took its toll on me.

TRANSPLANT

A WONDERFUL ORGANISATION CALLED UK Transplant matches organ donors with needy recipients. In the London area most helicopter operators are registered with UK Transplant, who call on them when they need one of the transplant teams to be moved around the country quickly. Two of the best-known hospitals specialising in transplants are Papworth in Cambridgeshire, and Harefield, which lies just inside the M25 on the north-west corner of London. Harefield is one of the largest and most experienced centres in the world for heart and lung transplants but at the time of my story in 1986 it was still a relatively new procedure. Christiaan Barnard was the first surgeon to perform a successful heart transplant in Cape Town, South Africa, in 1967; it was not until 1981 that a combined operation was carried out successfully to transplant both heart and lung. Two years later Harefield hospital performed their own first double transplant.

The advantage of a helicopter, of course, is that it can go door to door, whereas a fixed wing, albeit usually faster, has to use a runway and therefore involves at least two other forms of ground transport to achieve delivery. UK Transplant favoured the Agusta 109 because it was one of the fastest helicopters of its time in the world and would confidently sit in the cruise at up to 140 knots. With two engines it was also good for night flying and the cockpit had all the instrumentation and autopilot facilities needed for full certification under IFR (Instrument Flight Rules): the art of flying through cloud. (Having been a total dunce at flying on instruments at the start of my flying career, I had been determined to rectify the situation. By the time I left the Navy I had become an instructor in the subject.) I enjoyed the extra capability that the 109 gave us. Even on a fine day it was fun to plug in the autopilot with a deft flick of the fingers and then administer the flight by gentle adjustments to various knobs and switches instead of physically wrestling the machine along. It felt like being a grown-up aviator. The workload was actually higher but it kept the mind alert on otherwise long and laborious transit flights.

The previous day at Brands Hatch had been long but by no means dull. At that time the Grand Prix alternated each year between Silverstone and Brands. We preferred Silverstone because of the wide-open spaces and the old wartime airfield in the middle of the track; Brands Hatch was a different kettle of fish. The track itself lies in a steep-sided valley bowl so the helicopter 'airport', which for one day each year becomes statistically the busiest airport in the world, had to be located in a field at the top of the hill. The airborne shuttle to and from the Grand Prix was a heart-stopping exercise at the best of times but Brands raised the pucker factor by having a very tall row of electricity pylons across the end of the runway. This became yet another obstacle on a day when you were vying for the same tiny piece of airspace with 150 other helicopters. I seriously frightened myself there one year when I was departing to collect my next load of passengers from Battersea Heliport in central London. At about 200 feet I became aware of the sound of another helicopter. I can assure you that if you can actually hear another helicopter, he has to be very close. My head jerked from left to right and then above me and beneath me to try to find where the noise was coming from, but I dared not move a muscle to avoid the other machine for fear of going in the wrong direction and colliding with him. After what can only have been seconds, but which felt a hell of a lot longer than that, the culprit appeared in the Perspex panel beneath my feet, climbing much too fast and far too steeply. Once I knew where he was it was relatively easy to reduce my speed and increase my rate of climb, thus avoiding collision. I was positioned above and behind him, which meant there was no way that he'd seen me at all. He never knew how close he'd come to riding a rotor-less helicopter to the ground, and I went on to fly the rest of the day with all my senses dialled into self-preservation mode. But on Grand Prix day there's little time to dwell on incidents like this. The pressure of getting everybody in before race start and out before darkness descends lays claim to your full attention.

In 1986 the race at Brands was won by Nigel Mansell with five British drivers in the top five including Martin Brundell and Jonathon Palmer, whom I knew quite well as a fellow helicopter pilot. The big drama in that year was a first lap pile-up in which the French driver Jacques Lafitte broke both his legs. It was with quiet pride that I'd watched him being whisked away to hospital by my old Wessex 5 from 771 Squadron, there as the air ambulance in a Navy tradition I'd instigated seven years earlier.

The operational problem with Grand Prix Sunday is that all the pilots use up their legal 'duty hours' so that it's virtually impossible to find a pilot that can legally fly the day after. Thus it was that none of the London operators had a pilot available when the call came from UK Transplant on the Monday evening. Having spent the majority of Monday recovering from the 'Thank God we survived another

Grand Prix day' party at Fairoaks airfield in Surrey, I was planning to fly back home to Cornwall on the Tuesday morning. Events conspired to crown me as the only available pilot/helicopter combo available for work on Monday evening. My helicopter was already on the tarmac at Fairoaks so it didn't take long to flash her up and high-tail it over to Harefield, a short hop across the top of Heathrow.

I hadn't been to Harefield before but the regular flights by others meant that their landing pad was well marked and easy to find. The light was fading as I touched down just after 8pm but it was clear that it was going to be a still night with good visibility, just the sort of weather I like for night flying, which can be stressful at the best of times. I had been briefed to wait at the helipad until the eminent surgeon and his assistant arrived and then to take them to Taunton hospital in Somerset, a matter of about an hour's flying away, where they would extract the heart and lungs from a highly valued female donor who had lost her life in a road accident.

In chatting to the nurse who waited patiently at the helipad with me for the arrival of the surgeon, I learned two things. First, despite this transplant business being a relatively new craft, they were already performing over 800 operations a year. I was astonished at this since it still felt to me like something I'd only recently seen being heralded on television as a breakthrough. But what floored me was the fact that my two passengers, both surgeons, one female, had already performed two such operations since they had come on duty. Just to put that into perspective: it was a requirement that the removal and the insertion of the organs be performed by the same team. Without knowing anything about the subject I could see why this would be a good idea but staff shortages meant that this team had, so far, in the working 'day' done the following:

Driven to an airport.
Flown by fixed wing to Belgium.

Extracted a heart.

Flown back to London.

Driven to the hospital.

Inserted a heart.

Driven back to another airfield.

Flown chartered fixed wing to Scotland.

Extracted a heart.

Flown back to London.

Driven to the hospital.

Inserted their second heart.

So it was little surprise that having loaded their chilly-bins of special instruments into the rear of the helicopter, strapped themselves in and wolfed down the sandwiches that the operations department had laid on, they were both curled up on the seats and fast asleep by the time I'd started and lifted from Harefield.

It was a beautiful night flight down to Taunton. Two ambulances had been sensibly positioned with the beams of their headlights crossing at the 'H' where they wanted me to land. It was 10.30pm as our wheels touched down and my two passengers poured themselves a coffee from the thermos as I slowed the engines and rotors. I removed the two chilly-bins from the baggage compartment and began to carry them across the grass to the deserted hospital entrance, at which point the surgeon, who had obviously been here before, said, 'Look, it's pretty quiet here in the evenings. There's a television room with a coffee machine but I'm afraid it's in the sterile area'. I found myself scrubbing up and helping the surgeon on with his gown, just like you see in the movies. I naively tagged along behind him, carrying their bins of instruments, as he strode down the corridor and pushed through a double swing door into the well-lit operating room. I hadn't really been thinking ahead and was a bit surprised to find myself right next to an operating table with the donor laid out and 'prepared'.

'You're very welcome to stay and watch if you like but we could be anything up to four hours.'

I declined the offer (something I've often regretted as one of life's opportunities missed) and excused myself to find the coffee and television room. Apart from the activity in the operating room, the small country hospital was as quiet as the grave, and the irony of that expression was not lost on me at the time. I switched on the TV for the late news and was not altogether surprised to note that the BBC weather forecast was talking of overnight fog. There had been no mention of fog in the pre-flight forecast but the still winds on a summer night had increased the possibility soon after we'd departed from Harefield.

Normally I'd have grabbed a bit of shut-eye at this point but I was acutely aware of the need to get going as soon as the organ removal was complete and I would have been highly embarrassed to have been found asleep by two people who had clearly had a much longer day than me. So I made a couple of phone calls to forecasters I trusted and although there were pockets of fog beginning to appear around the south-west of the country it didn't look like big trouble brewing. I settled in to watch a few hours of dreadful TV programming well past the witching hour. At one point I idly glanced out of the window towards where the helicopter was parked and was horrified to note it had disappeared. A thick blanket had descended on Taunton.

Perhaps surprisingly, fog is not an absolute deterrent to take-off in a suitably equipped helicopter. It takes a bit of nerve but you can ascend vertically, albeit blind, until you pop out of the top and can begin to transition to forward flight. A fog layer, however dense, rarely rises more than a couple of hundred feet above the ground when it forms in the valleys on a still evening. The problem arises on landing, where a helicopter simply doesn't have the sophisticated equipment to permit a fully automated descent into a fog bank. So my attention, and another couple of phone calls, focused on the destination at Harefield rather than the departure from Taunton and the conditions en route.

I let myself back into the operating room and waited quietly until the surgeon noticed I was there. I wanted to ask where his parameters lay since the possibility of not being able to fly him, and of course the organs, back to Harefield had begun to rear its head. I wasn't sure whether that had any bearing on how he now viewed the operation. With his elbows deep inside a chest cavity he reassured me that they would press on towards conclusion regardless, and if I had to throw away the flight they would get a flashing-blue-light escort by road. The longer journey back would reduce the chances of a successful transplant but he kindly recognised that when it comes to weather it is what it is. (I say 'kindly' because I've had many passengers who do not acknowledge this simple fact and think that it's the fault of the pilot.)

About an hour later the operation was complete and we were ready to depart. I made one more quick phone call to ensure that the fog hadn't yet settled in to Harefield and that I had a couple of alternative destinations to aim for if it did. With that done we loaded up.

'Do you mind strapping this chilly-bin into the co-pilot's seat this time?' asked the surgeon.

'Sure I can. Why's that?' I responded.

'Because it contains the organs.' Ah.

With everything running and ready to go I took a deep breath, checked the instruments, reminded myself of what I was going to do in the event of various possible problems and then pulled smoothly up to full power. Taunton hospital just disappeared... one... two... three... and the night sky appeared as we came up out of the fog like a cork out of a bottle. It was as if Taunton had never existed. The sudden change in visual landscape was quite unsettling. I pushed the nose gently forward and we began to accelerate and climb to our cruise altitude. I levelled out at a comfortable 5,000 feet, which feels like space travel in a helicopter, and turned around to check that my passengers were happy. They were both fast asleep again in the faint warm glow from the overhead reading lights.

I settled into my seat for a solo flight. Except that it wasn't really solo for beside me in the co-pilot's seat was a human heart. It had finished its role with one life and was on its way to a role with another, propelled by me. It was an eerie feeling, not a bad one at all, just a little challenging, and it felt somehow momentous. One of those snapshot moments you carry with you for ever after.

As the heart and I continued on our journey towards London, the landscape beneath us became one of the most beautiful night tableaus I have ever seen before or since. If the masters of film illusions had created it, you would think it too unreal. Above us the full moon and insanely bright stars cast silver light downwards. Below us about sixty per cent of the land was crisply seen in the moonlight with hedges and fields clearly visible. But in the valleys the fog stood out in thick patches, again illuminated by the moon. Within most of those patches lay a hamlet, a town or, in the case of Salisbury, an entire city, blanketed, invisible and asleep. Sodium street lights illuminated the fog bank from within, giving the only clue to the life that lay under the blanket. I felt a distinct link between what I was seeing outside the aircraft and the human heart that sat patiently beside me as my co-pilot. It was a seminal moment in my flying career.

We landed safely, the team disembarked and disappeared inside the hospital only an hour or two before the sun was due to rise. As with so many of the rescues I'd performed in the Navy I never did find out the result of the operation, nor where 'my' heart was destined for. I took off back to Fairoaks feeling good but humbled.

BREAKING THINGS

AEROPLANE PILOTS REGARD THEIR flying machines as elegant doves that soar effortlessly on a warm breeze and gilded wings. By and large an aeroplane will glide, often some considerable distance, when the engine fails, and there are very few failures catastrophic enough to wrench them from the sky. A helicopter pilot, on the other hand, accepts that his machine is an intricate intermeshing of mechanical components, any number of which can cause heart-stopping moments.

The rotors are no more than thin and flexible wings but they must be constantly propelled in a circle by at least one, often two, and sometimes as many as three engines. It's pretty rare to get a failure of a rotor blade although the slightest change in shape, just a thin layer of ice for example, can dramatically change the way the blade travels through the air, causing violent vibrations through the airframe. Ice is a notorious enemy of the helicopter since it can build up on the blades so insidiously. When flying through cold and damp air it's likely that ice builds up evenly across all the blades and you only become aware of trouble when a small piece breaks away and puts one blade out of balance. We've all experienced ice to some extent and we learn to give it a wide berth and plenty of respect. My own experience was pretty benign. On a routine training flight in the rescue Wessex I descended from an area of relatively cold, dry air into very wet and slightly warmer air. As the warmer air hit the cold airframe it turned instantly to ice and the windscreen became opaque. This wasn't a huge problem in itself since I was able to slow down and lean my head out of the combined door/window, albeit catching icicles on my face. But the fact that ice was forming quickly on the windscreen was a good indication that it was surely doing the same on the blades, so I put out a Pan call and gingerly landed in the nearest field to wait for the airframe to warm up just a degree or two and be able to continue without gaining more ice. It made the local newspaper that week but didn't really qualify as a big problem as it had been such an obvious problem and solution.

Before we go any further, let me put to rest one of the most common misconceptions about a helicopter. When the engine or engines fail it does not fall out of the sky. The Sycamore tree sheds its seeds to the ground, each attached to a single 'rotor blade'. As the seed falls, the rush of air coming up at it spins the rotor blade and it floats gently towards the earth. So it is with a helicopter. Normally the engines are using brute force to turn the rotor blades, which in turn generates lift. But sometimes the engines stop providing the service, when the fuel runs out or through some kind of mechanical failure. When that happens the pilot encourages the helicopter to descend and it becomes a huge Sycamore seed. The air rushes upwards as the helicopter drops and the blades keep turning as a result. When the ground is getting close there is enough momentum in the blades for the pilot to convert it to lift and use it to safely alight on the surface.

The catch is that you only get one go at it before all the momentum is exhausted from the blades, so it's a good idea to time it right. It's not good to make your 'landing' 20 feet above the ground because the blades then have no energy left in them and you know the last 19 feet will be spent in a plummet. Every six months or so all helicopter pilots go flying with an instructor and practise the technique of 'autorotation', or 'autos', until an engine failure is no longer a thing to fear.

I've had three engine failures in my flying career so far. Two of these were in single-engined helicopters, but with the first there was no time for an auto. It was three years after I'd left the Navy. I had been working in the London area and popped into the old Brooklands motor-racing track at Weybridge, which served as the base for Air Hanson, probably the most prominent helicopter operator in the UK at the time. This visit was partly to see a few old mates for a coffee and partly to collect some fuel for my return trip to Cornwall, a trip of only a couple of hours. While I took a look at the weather details en route, one of the ever enthusiastic and efficient Air Hanson ground crew fuelled my Longranger helicopter. All start-up checks completed, I lifted into a hover of around 10 feet and air-taxied away from the fuel pumps. As I did so I was glancing at the instrument panel to check that all were in good shape before accelerating and climbing away to the west. But one instrument, designed to indicate the internal running temperature of the small jet engine, didn't seem to be in good shape at all. Instead of showing something around 700°C TOT (Turbine Outlet Temperature), it was suggesting that it was operating at around half that figure. This would be impossible, since there wouldn't be enough power coming out of the engine to continue to drive the rotors at full speed, and therefore was probably why the 10 feet between me and the ground had diminished to half that height and why the helicopter's next move was to very politely and gently settle on to the tarmac.

Just as I was thinking that that was a very strange thing, the engine stopped completely. It transpired that the chap who'd refuelled me had diligently carried out all the usual checks that morning, including draining some fuel into a glass jar from the bottom of the airfield storage tank and checking that it was clear. This was to ensure that no water was present in the fuel. It certainly had been clear but he'd missed doing the additional chemical check that would have told him it was clear because it was *all* water. The ground crewman was mortified to discover that about forty gallons of the stuff had found its way into the tank overnight and most of it had been transferred to my Longranger. So, on reflection, my poor helicopter had done rather well to get us airborne at all. It would be another 24 hours before the engineers could be confident that they'd flushed every drop of water out of the system and I could continue on my way. Every time I returned to Brooklands thereafter I always asked for the same guy to refuel me. I knew that at the sight of me approaching he would always double-check every last potential for a slip-up and, after all, no harm had been done.

My other engine failure in a single-engined helicopter was a less gentle affair but was also in a civilian helicopter, about ten years later, in a slightly smaller Jetranger. We had spent about six months stripping down and rebuilding a low-time (the air equivalent of low mileage) import from the USA. We'd christened her with the registration G-HELE and she gleamed like new in every detail. (All British flying machines start with a G, followed by four letters. You can have any combination of letters provided it's never been used before and isn't offensive. The only time I've heard of an application being rejected was when Prince William of Gloucester wanted a registration that went with his initials.) G-HELI had been taken many years earlier, so G-HELE it was.

Mick Wright was an engineer from Air Hanson I'd taken on as chief engineer at Castle Air. When I'd left to start another company,

Helifilms, he stayed with me and we've been together ever since. When Mick gives up engineering, I'm giving up flying. He is the most diligent engineer you could ever come across but with an entirely balanced and pragmatic judgement on whether a given sign of trouble is safe or not to go flying with. He's been watching my six o'clock for nearly thirty years now and as we've grown older together we've hopefully both grown a little wiser.

The day in question was the very first day we'd used G-HELE commercially since the rebuild, and I was airborne over a power station at Didcot in Oxfordshire, filming the extent of the huge cooling towers and other assets there on behalf of an advertising agency. Thankfully only the cameraman and myself were on location for the very simple shoot when I decided it might look nice if we flew straight across the top of the only brick chimney that didn't have smoke or steam billowing from it. The shot did indeed look great as we flew low across the lip of the giant and cavernous chimney, but just before we reached the other lip there was a very loud pop and the engine simply shut itself down. There was just enough forward momentum for me to convert speed into height and we hopped over the outer lip with only a few feet to spare.

G-HELE, despite no longer having an engine to run the rotors, responded beautifully to my request for autorotation and everything was going well. But of course a power station is completely surrounded by power lines, many of which criss-crossed the short 300-foot gap between me and the ground. Over one set, under another, over a third and within less than ten seconds I was pulling up the collective lever to cushion our landing on the grass. As the rotors ran down the cameraman and I looked at each other in astonishment that a) we'd survived the wires and b) that the engine had failed at all. Opening the doors we looked back towards 'our' cooling tower and could clearly see from our new position on the ground that there may not have been visible smoke or steam emanating from it but something was making the air shimmer. Whatever that something was, it obviously didn't have enough oxygen in it to feed a hungry jet engine, and I knew the 'pop' I'd heard was entirely in keeping with a compressor stall, exactly what you get if you starve an engine of oxygen.

Feeling chastened and hugely embarrassed at my own stupidity, I restarted the engine, checked it out for a few minutes on the ground and then gingerly tried a hover. As suspected, the engine was running beautifully, and we were able to finish the task and return Mick's pride and joy to him without a scratch. Only my pride was dented.

In the thirty years I've just mentioned there has only been one occasion on which Mick has made the slightest error. Thankfully it was funny enough to report here, and in due course Mick will forgive me for doing so. Another filming task in G-HELE had taken us to London Docklands. That morning Mick had completed some work on the hydraulic system at our base, while being pressurised by me to be ready in time for the allotted task. Almost all helicopters no longer have direct mechanical linkages from pilot to rotors; the control is effected via a series of hydraulic jacks that take the physical load away from the pilot and turn what would otherwise be a strenuous exercise into a light and precise form of flying controls. In broad terms these consist of a collective lever in your left hand that lifts the helicopter up and down, a cyclic control in your right hand that tips the rotors in the direction you want to travel, and two yaw pedals that control which way the nose of the helicopter is pointing. A failure of the hydraulic system is another thing we practise by simply switching it off, at which point all the controls become extremely heavy. This sort of failure would normally be caused by a leak from the hydraulic fluid system, but there's a good amount of fluid in reserve and you have to lose enormous amounts of it to affect the control system.

I met the film director in the Docklands at the appointed hour, strapped him securely into the rear cabin of G-HELE and began work with the cameraman, who was sitting beside me in the

front cockpit. We stuck to the line of the River Thames, as all single-engined helicopters are required to do. In this way they can be sure of having somewhere to go in the event of an emergency without fear of injuring third parties on the ground in the busy city. The shot the director requested was a simple forward-looking progression along the Thames that said 'This is London', a shot we had done many times before (and since). The director had a TV monitor in the back and declared himself happy with our work after only the second run along the river. It was only a short five minute trip back to the east where we would drop the director in the Docklands and continue home to our base. But as I made all the usual radio calls and turned over Albert Bridge to return to the Docklands I had the distinct impression that the controls were becoming heavier.

After a few tentative experiments I confirmed that the hydraulic system was indeed failing. I put out a Pan call. Our Docklands landing site (long before they built London City Airport there) was still the closest point to land and I started to make my way gingerly there. The controls were becoming heavier by the minute but regular practice meant it wasn't something to be feared, it would just make the final touchdown – always a bit tricky in a helicopter – much harder to achieve gently. But gentle it was and once on the ground I slowed the engine to the idle setting to allow the usual two-minute cool-down period before stopping the engine and rotors completely. This gave me a moment to turn around in my seat to apologise to the director for frightening him.

'Oh my God!' I exclaimed. The poor chap patiently sat there with his hair slicked down over his face by gallons of hot red sticky hydraulic fluid that was then dripping off his chin into a large puddle in which his feet and ruined shoes were resting.

'I am *so* sorry,' I stuttered. 'How long has it been doing *that*?'

'Oh, pretty much since we took off,' he politely responded.

'But why didn't you say something?'

'I thought it must always be like this in the back of a helicopter.'

I couldn't think of a suitable response to that one.

It only took a quick glance to see that I'd pressurised Mick just a little too hard to finish the work on time and that the final tightening of one of the hydraulic pipe connections had been missed. As I said, we're a bit older and a bit wiser now.

The only mechanical failure I suffered in a naval aircraft happened over Malta. We were on a tour of the Mediterranean in HMS *Hermes* and I was flying as co-pilot to Bob Barton, one of those pilots who is not only a great aviator but backs it up with detailed technical knowledge. He later went on to become the harbour master in Guernsey, which I thought was a loss to aviation.

Hermes was tied up alongside the wharf in Valletta harbour and most of the squadron were ashore getting some R&R, but we'd been assigned to a test flight before we could join them in the sunshine. There were few facilities on board for opening up a helicopter engine in the event of a problem so the standard procedure was to change the entire engine and let the workshops back in the UK solve the problem. The test flight following an engine change generally took about an hour and a half and, to me, was a remarkably boring exercise involving flying the helicopter through various flight parameters and carefully noting down the temperatures, pressures and power readings. We were accompanied by the squadron engineering officer who was standing behind the pilots' seats when the brand new engine blew up.

The engines on a Sea King, as with most helicopters other than the Wessex, are just above and behind the pilot's head. A tiny metal fracture had caused a small turbine blade, no bigger than a thumbnail, to depart the engine. Since a turbine (or jet) is rotating at about 96,000 rpm, you can imagine that a departing blade is travelling at something not far below supersonic and certainly behaves like a bullet. As we later discovered it had exited straight down and only narrowly avoided drilling down through the top of the engineer's head by virtue of hitting a solid control box about the size of two cigarette packets and bouncing back up.

The noise alone was enough to cause Bob to shut down the engine but the instruments were already showing that this engine had no interest in continuing its participation in this flight. Of course, we didn't know the cause of the problem at that moment, but the air traffic controller at Luqa, the international airport, did call us to ask if we knew we had smoke and flames trailing behind us into the clear blue sky over Malta. We declared an emergency and headed to the airport while I pulled the big red handle that would inject fire retardant into the engine bay. If a fire stays confined to within the engine then there's not too much of a problem, but once it spreads towards the second engine and various other essential items it does get more interesting. The fire extinguisher evidently did its job as the control tower could no longer see flames, only smoke, trailing out behind us.

A nice long runway is a good idea when only running on one engine. In some circumstances you can come to a hover on one engine if the helicopter is very light but there's no point in putting more strain on the good engine than absolutely necessary and a helicopter flying forwards uses considerably less power than one in the hover. The runway was a huge expanse of concrete, the fire trucks had all lined up to meet us and Bob knew exactly what he was doing so, apart from calling out a few power parameters in order that he could continue to concentrate on the flying task, I had time to enjoy the drama of the moment. Bob landed the helicopter beautifully and having successfully restrained the Maltese fire fighters from covering us in foam we were able to abandon the Sea King to the care of the engineering officer and hurry off to regale our compatriots in the bar with increasingly lurid details of how we'd battled the forces of darkness and come out on top.

The worst card a helicopter ever dealt me was a tail rotor failure, which neatly and directly joined together the experience learned in the Navy with survival in civilian flying. The job of the tail rotor is to stop the aircraft from spinning on its own axis. Any sort of problem involving the tail rotor sends a shiver down the spine of every helicopter pilot. You can't practise it in the real world so the best you can do is to talk about it a lot, listen carefully to anybody who has suffered the problem, and read all the post-accident reports you can lay your hands on.

When two powerful engines and a gearbox are constantly working to push heavy rotor blades through the air, the blades are resisting and trying to turn the helicopter in the opposite direction. This is known as torque and is why the tail rotor is more correctly referred to as the 'anti-torque' rotor. Without one, the main rotor blades would still turn but the body of the helicopter would end up spinning the other way. The results of failure of the tail rotor while a helicopter is in a high hover will almost always be fatal unless the pilot has the presence of mind to shut down the engines within one or two seconds. If it happens to you in forward flight, however, you're in with a chance as the big shark's fin at the back of the tail helps to work against the air and keep you from spinning. It won't keep the nose of the aircraft pointing in the way you're travelling but it will stop it from beginning the spin. The catch is that once you slow down your forward speed (in order to land), the air over the tail reduces, it becomes less effective and eventually the spin begins.

So, if the tail rotor itself breaks up, or if the long and slender driveshaft that powers it should break, there are only two options. You can immediately shut down your engines and give yourself about twenty seconds to learn to fly a new sort of flying machine before it meets the earth, or you can buy yourself some thinking time by keeping up your forward speed and letting the big tail fin compensate. But eventually you're going to have to make a landing, by which time you'd better have a good plan in place.

I'd only once met a crew who'd experienced the problem. While still flying Sea Kings on anti-submarine work the squadron had been flying from HMS *Hermes* to the south of Portland. The crew in question had suffered a fracture in the tail rotor driveshaft and had gone for the option of continuing to fly forward. The Sea King had wheels so you could make your fast approach to a runway until eventually, just before touch down, you had to stop the engines to allow the nose of the helicopter to point along the runway just at the moment the wheels touched the ground. If you didn't do that then you'd hit the runway going fast and partially sideways. This would result in rolling the helicopter at high speed, a manoeuvre unlikely to be survivable.

When we eventually met up again with the crew in the bar that evening we crowded around them asking question after question. What was the first indication? What did it feel like? How far round did the nose come when the failure happened? How slowly could you go before feeling she would spin? How low were you when you cut the engines? Would you do the same again next time? And so on and so on. All this information contributed to saving my life over a decade later.

I was flying our Agusta 109, a beautiful sleek Ferrari of a helicopter that could carry seven passengers faster than most others. I loved flying the 109, not least because it – unusually – had a very comfortable pilot's seat. You could spend eight hours flying and still get out of the cockpit unaided and without the need for an immediate visit to a chiropractor. I had been working for about eight weeks on a documentary called *Landshapes* about the geology of the British Isles. It was an innovative programme in so far as being almost continuously shot from the air. For most of the shoot I'd used a single-engined Jetranger. It was lighter, cheaper to operate and better for low-level filming work, but the last part of the documentary related the story of the mountains on the Isle of Skye. The need to travel over the sea and the need to work in the high mountains dictated that the two engines in a 109 would be the sensible choice.

After a full day of filming I was on my way back down to southern England. If we hurried we could just about make it back before darkness, not essential but a good idea when we were all pretty tired and the weather was unpredictable. The cameraman, Chris Cox, was fast asleep in the rear cabin surrounded by the tools of his trade. He'd spent most of the day hanging out of the open door operating a Tyler mount, a wonderful contraption of heavy metal that we used to help stabilise the camera before the days of the sophisticated gyro-stabilised Cineflex mounts that we use now. It was a physical and tiring job for him at the best of times but he'd additionally been out in the freezing cold airstream and rotor downwash for a lot of the day so he was curled up in his ski suit and sleeping the sleep of the just. The producer/director was Tim Fell who had devised the documentary series and had put full trust in me to organise all the logistics and permissions we needed to achieve the shoot. Thank heaven he had chosen to fly back sitting next to me in the co-pilot's seat, as I was shortly going to need his help.

We were at about 5,000 feet over the bleak Pennine Hills of Yorkshire when there was an almighty bang and the nose of the helicopter slewed around to the right by about 30 or 40 degrees. I instantly knew in my heart what the problem was and the first question was: 'Are we still capable of flying?' It was uncomfortable, it was scary, and it was an unnatural way to be flying, but she seemed to be coping. We were rolled over on one side to the extent that I was looking down at Tim on my left but things weren't getting any worse than they had been in that first violent manoeuvre at the moment the tail rotor driveshaft had sheared.

Two quite extraordinary things happened, both of which will live with me for ever. They used to say about Ayrton Senna, the great racing driver, that his brain worked much faster than the rest of us. Most other drivers returned to the pits and simply reported that the car had behaved well through a particular corner, but Ayrton was renowned for being able to give a step-by-step description in great detail of how the tyres, the suspension and the aerodynamics had worked through each section of the corner. When you consider the speeds he was doing and that it only took a second or two to negotiate a corner you can begin to understand the amount of information his brain was assimilating, then processing and committing to memory. When my driveshaft sheared I experienced the same phenomenon. If you'd asked me only seconds earlier to relate everything I knew about tail rotors I would have stumbled and stuttered and mumbled a few disconnected facts, but at the instant of failure my brain speeded up to a flash of lightning that I have never experienced before or since. I very meticulously remembered everything I'd ever read, heard or talked about relating to tail rotors. I instantly recalled every nuance of that bar conversation with my Navy pals over a decade earlier. I discarded any information that was peripheral or inappropriate to my own circumstances, then sorted the remaining items into priority order and made a plan. It's hard to know exactly how long that took but in discussing it among ourselves some time later I reckon it took something under two seconds. As Tim put it, 'I couldn't believe how instinctively you knew what to do and began to do it.'

No, Tim, nor could I.

The second extraordinary phenomenon was how long it took me to shake the belief that I'd caused the problem. There were few ways that I could have done. About the only thing I could think of was if I'd left one of the cowlings unlatched during my pre-flight inspection and it had blown off and taken the tail rotor with it. This thought kept coming back to the forefront of my mind, accompanied by a very real fear of peer ridicule at the subsequent enquiry. This far outweighed any fear of injury or death and I had to take a firm decision to put it out of my mind as whatever had caused the thing didn't now matter and I had to use all available brain power to deal with the consequences and aftermath. (Eventually I would learn that it was a pure metallurgical fracture that had been latent since manufacture, so my fears were unfounded.)

Having established that we were still airborne and capable of remaining that way, my next move was to put out a Mayday call and declare my intention to make my way towards Teesside airport. Not only was this the nearest civilian airfield with a tarmac runway but it was well equipped with fire and emergency services in the event that I turned this flying machine into a small bonfire. But it was still a good twenty minutes' flying away so I had good time available to put the rest of the plan in place. Chris was, of course, now wide awake and I asked him to spend the time ensuring that everything in the rear cabin – cameras, camera mount and any other loose articles, however small – was very firmly strapped down. The last thing we wanted at the critical moment was to have a lot of loose metal flying around our ears. Next I asked the air traffic controller to put in a phone call to base and advise Mick, my engineering partner, of the predicament I was in. I've no idea why I did this other than some half-formed thought that he would soon have to drive up to Teesside, whatever the outcome. He still raises his eyes to the heavens when reminded that I put him through the next twenty terrifying minutes, despite there being nothing whatsoever he could do about it to help me from 250 miles away.

I received two offers of help, first from a big Sikorsky 76 helicopter that was inbound to his base on the Yorkshire coast from an oil rig out in the North Sea. I gladly accepted his offer to fly towards me and he appeared about halfway through the journey to Teesside. There's no way you can see your own tail from the cockpit and I was keen to learn what it looked like back there as it would, to a certain extent, dictate what I could expect to experience in the latter stages of the approach to the runway. If I'd left a cowling open and the tail rotor had been ripped away entirely, which I still believed was a possibility, then the effect could be marginally different to that if the driveshaft had simply sheared and left the static tail rotor assembly attached. But most importantly I was anxious to learn whether there had been any damage to the big fin. If that too was about to fail then I would need to be ready for an instantaneous engine shutdown and autorotation to earth. Thankfully everything looked intact to the Sikorsky pilot as he manoeuvred around the rear of my helicopter in close formation and took a good squint at all the detail. He kindly offered to stay with me until the end and I was frankly glad of his moral support. There was nothing he could do to help and he didn't bother me with any unnecessary radio calls, but I was very glad he was there.

The second offer of help came from Tim Fell sitting next to me.

At first glance this was a somewhat ludicrous offer made out of a feeling of helplessness at a time when I was clearly well loaded up with tasks. However, I took the opportunity to brief both Tim and Chris quite thoroughly on the sequence of events they could expect from here on. I didn't pull any punches about the scale of the problem but I did avoid mentioning that my accelerated sifting of available knowledge had reminded me that the last 109 crew to suffer the same problem, in Germany earlier that year, had rolled the helicopter down the runway at high speed and had all perished.

As I was working my way through describing the critical actions I'd be taking during the final approach I realised that I was going to run out of hands at exactly the wrong moment. The engine throttles, and shutdown valves, were positioned in the overhead panel just above my left ear, but at the very instant I was going to be needing to shut down the engines I would be only 10 feet above the runway and would need my left hand on the collective lever to time the moment of 'kissing' the tarmac precisely. I therefore spent the next few minutes briefing Tim on how to operate the throttles and shut down the engines. He listened intently and we ran through it a second time to confirm the commands I would give and when he could expect them. So his offer of help was not in vain after all.

The last part of the journey down from the hills towards the airport were used to experiment with the flight envelope of this new and strange flying machine without a tail rotor. I had to plant my feet firmly and consciously on the floor to avoid automatically trying to use the now useless yaw pedals. I needed to select the speed at which I would make my final approach. Too fast and the potential for drama increased, too slow and we ran the risk of beginning to spin or at least the risk of flying so unnaturally sideways that a survivable landing would be extremely difficult to achieve. I eventually settled on around 60 knots.

By this time the light was beginning to fade and we could easily see the terminal lights of the airport in the middle distance. We were not yet lined up with the runway so the view of the airport was not yet dominated by the runway lights. Instead our eyes were inevitably drawn to the blue flashing lights of a good dozen emergency vehicles lined up beside the runway threshold, ready to follow us down the runway and deal with the aftermath. I had talked with the air traffic controller about the option for laying a foam runway, a procedure used when fire is highly likely to break out, such as when an airliner is landing with its wheels up. We'd decided between us to dispense with that option since it had the potential to introduce new problems if the runway was wet and there was foam flying around in the turbulence from the rotors.

As the runway lights began to line up in the gathering gloom I eased the nose around to the left on to my final approach. The speed was nicely holding to the allocated 60 knots, we were fully briefed and all knew what we were about to do. I made the standard 'finals' call on the radio, perhaps a little superfluous as all other traffic had been cleared away from the airport and all airport eyes were already looking in our direction. The Sikorsky pilot peeled away from the station he'd been holding alongside me and simply called 'Good luck' on the radio.

I felt suddenly very alone, as if I were drowning and somebody had just let go of my hand.

It didn't happen quickly, it happened slowly. The runway lights gradually grew bigger in the windscreen and I had too much time to wonder if there was anything I'd forgotten, if there was something I should be doing differently. And then we were over the threshold, the blue flashing lights had passed behind our left-hand window and there was only the ground left to meet.

I didn't try to arrest the shallow descent I'd initiated. I didn't want to change any of the characteristics that had served well up to that point. I'd briefed that we would chop the engines at 10 feet above the runway but as we passed through 10 feet something held me back until half that height. Our nose was still a good 30 degrees off runway heading but I left it until about 5 feet before calling, 'SHUTDOWN.' Tim neatly, quietly and efficiently brought both engine controls back to idle, released the gate that was designed to prevent inadvertent engine shutdown, and pulled the levers fully aft. As the engines disconnected their drive to the rotors the nose of the helicopter swung violently and rapidly to the left. I was glad I'd left it until later as there was only just enough time to descend through the last 5 feet and get the wheels on to the ground before the nose would otherwise have swung past the runway heading and we would have been lost.

The wheels touched firmly but not heavily and every nerve ending in my body was straining to feel the slightest nuance of what the aircraft was doing. In horror I could feel the right wheel come up into the air again as the other two wheels struggled against the spinning momentum and screeched against the tarmac. The rotors were still turning but would not have much effect as they slowed; never the less I held the cyclic control over to full right and just held my breath. As the speed fell below 50 knots the right wheel decided it would rejoin the tarmac after all and we were finally down. I gently applied the foot brakes, she slowed to a stop and I applied the rotor brake to induce silence in everything. In unison the three of us exhaled very slowly and very deeply.

As the big airfield fire trucks arrived alongside us, together with an ambulance and some extra fire appliances that had been called in from the city fire brigade, we firmly shook hands with each other and looked one another in the eye and nodded. There wasn't really anything to be said for the moment – that would come later in the bar as we talked and talked into the night (and into a bottle of scotch) to exorcise the demons. We just opened the doors and took a deep lungful of Yorkshire seaside air. It was an immense surprise that I couldn't make it all the way from the cockpit door to the rear of the helicopter to take a look at the tail. I wasn't shaking and my legs didn't give way or anything so dramatic, I just needed desperately to sit for a moment on the tarmac. I looked up at the chief fireman and said, 'Look, I know we're in the middle of an airport runway and everything, but I'm going to light up a cigarette, OK?'

'You go right ahead, mate,' he kindly responded.

EMMA

WHEN FLYING RESCUE WORK professionally it's possible and necessary to remain detached from the human drama unfolding beneath the aircraft. People are injured, people die, people are saved and the overriding concern is whether we exercised full professionalism throughout the operation. Occasionally you might react passionately to an event, such as when the young boys were lost in the aircraft ditching on the day that our divers had been withdrawn. If any technique could be improved, even slightly, then it might save just one more life in the years that followed and so we were hard on ourselves and hard on our team mates if we ever felt there was room for improvement. But in terms of the people we lifted we only recorded their names for the sake of the paperwork and our lives only touched theirs for just a few minutes, albeit probably their most significant few minutes ever. It was therefore more than ironic, and perhaps a closing of the circle, that the last time I ever took part in a Search and Rescue operation was the first time I ever had a pre-existing relationship with the victim.

When we started Castle Air we were happy to employ our helicopters on just about any revenue-earning task and in the course of first looking for work we were introduced to the warden and manager of Lundy Island, a rocky outcrop and the largest island in the Bristol Channel. Lundy was and still is a rather eccentric British institution with a chequered past. It lies just twelve miles off the Devon coast, measures three miles by three-quarters of a mile and gives its name to one of the British sea areas used in the shipping forecast. In fact, it's the sea area that adjoins Fastnet.

The name Lundy is said to mean Puffin Island in old Norse; highly appropriate in view of the number of birds of the same name who used to alight and breed there and which are just beginning to make a comeback. Inscriptions on stones in the island's cemetery date back to the 5th century AD. Island history includes lurid tales of piracy, disputed ownership and dramatic shipwrecks throughout the centuries. In 1969 the island was put up for sale and caused apoplexy among traditionalists when it was rumoured that it might become an offshore tax and gambling haven. In the end a British millionaire named Jack Hayward bought the island and gave it to the National Trust in the interests of the nation. But the catch is that the National Trust are unable to take on projects that are not financially self-supporting so it was duly leased to the Landmark Trust.

The Landmark Trust set about making the island a fully functioning and self-supporting tourist destination and soon succeeded in this tremendous task by virtue of good management and the sensitive restoration of the eleven properties on the island, all of which can be stayed in as holiday rents. During the summer months the island's own ship carries visitors from the ports of Bideford and Ilfracombe, but the problem in the winter months was that the high seas usually precluded landings at a time when birdwatching enthusiasts and those seeking an isolated break still wanted to visit. Our first major commission at Castle Air was to ferry visitors back and forth to the island from the nearest point of land at Hartland Point. We set up a little helipad on top of the windswept clifftop and positioned an old caravan there to sleep in on a Saturday night.

The Landmark Trust is a private trust set up by Sir John and Lady Smith, a remarkable couple with great vision who found a way to buy and restore buildings or locations with historical or architectural merit and then offer them for holiday rental. Founded in 1965, the trust has around 190 properties. Sir John, now deceased, came from a banking dynasty and was a director of, among other things, Coutts private bank for over forty years. He also numbered many other accomplishments such as being a director of Rolls Royce, a Member of Parliament and the Lord-Lieutenant of Berkshire. But he was one of my personal heroes as a result of having been an observer in the Royal Navy, flying in Swordfish, Barracudas and Avengers. His was one of three aircraft that attacked the German battleship *Tirpitz* in 1944.

Soon after we started the shuttle flights to Lundy I was pleased to meet Sir John's son Barty, who was also an aviation enthusiast and a very good helicopter pilot himself. We went on to become firm friends over the years, sharing a love of helicopters and motor racing. (Barty was also to become something of a patron to me in subsequent aviation projects and for many years we shared a helicopter between us. He provided the capital and I provided the ongoing operational costs until my emigration to Australia in 2002.)

At the time in question Barty had been tasked with overseeing the growth of Lundy Island as a destination and took an enormous personal interest in every detail. The Smith family had five children but it was Barty and his youngest sister Emma who particularly felt a deep personal connection with the island and would often fly over with us. On occasions they would remain for a few days longer than expected and we would be asked to come and pick them up when they were ready to return.

So it was that on Wednesday 9 November in 1983 I rang Barty at 9.30am to ask if he and Emma still wanted picking up and bringing back to the mainland that morning. His response that they had 'lost' Emma sent a shiver down my spine. Emma had set out for a walk around the island the previous evening but by 6pm had failed to return. Being dark by then the level of concern rapidly rose and the RAF were asked to begin a search for her using their well-equipped yellow Sea King out of the nearby base at Chivenor. All the islanders had set out to search in lines, calling out to Emma. By the time I rang Barty on the Wednesday morning the RAF had also been airborne all night and failed to find her. I told Barty I would be there right away and alerted Roy Flood, who I knew would be equally concerned and would want to come.

Roy and I set off in great trepidation knowing that the fact that the RAF had failed to locate Emma during an all-night operation meant that this situation was unlikely to have a happy outcome. From our base to the island was a flight of about 30 minutes. I took the time to brief Roy on how we would set about the search, how we would divide up the cockpit responsibilities and what we would do in any number of possible outcomes. Roy visibly paled and it was the only time in ten years of working together that I ever saw him in any way unsure of himself.

We landed at our usual spot, next to the windswept church on the highest point of the island, and Barty immediately climbed into the rear of the Jetranger. We were using G-SPEY, a really beautiful helicopter in dark green with two gold stripes. It had been originally owned by the proprietor of the Spey whiskey distillery in Scotland and he had stylishly fitted it out to match his Rolls Royce. The seats were thus in beautiful soft tan leather and it actually featured a small drinks cabinet. This was all a far cry from the helicopters I had been used to using on SAR work and, of course, there was no rescue winch fitted, but the real issue was that all the fancy interior rendered it a very heavy machine for any hovering work close to the cliffs.

We took a two-minute brief from Barty in which we learned that the RAF crew had been airborne again at first light but were currently breakfasting at their base while their Sea King was refuelled. Barty described Emma's intentions and the likely route that she would have taken on her walk. We knew that the powerful lights of the Sea King had covered all the surface area of the island quite thoroughly through the night and so I decided to begin our own search by covering the rocky 300-foot cliffs that surrounded the island. I took a moment to brief Roy and Barty on how a casualty always looks much smaller than your eyes expect it to appear.

These cliffs were almost sheer at every point around the island. A good deal of turbulence was created as the westerly winds encountered the enormous rock walls for the first time since departing the eastern shores of America, over 3,000 miles away. But this day was almost unique in being perfectly still. I climbed up from the island and then curved to the right and down to descend below island height and begin our search of the cliffs.

Within what seemed like only seconds but was certainly less than five minutes, suddenly there was Emma. She was sitting very peacefully, just above sea level, with her back to the cliffs looking out across the ocean, or so it seemed at first. As I circled around in order to be able to hover closer there was no sign of a response from Emma, no wave to us, nor even a sign of movement. I banished terrible thoughts of how she might have got there and concentrated on putting the helicopter into a position whereby either Barty and/or Roy could exit the helicopter and go to Emma on foot. There was really only one place where I had any chance of doing this and that would involve employing the technique I had practised for so many years on the Camel's Head. I would have to continue to hover but place the corner of one of the skids in a position where it was touching a small rock just above the water. If I took it gently I figured Roy would just about be able to climb out of the front seat, stand on the skid and then transfer his weight to the rock. I say 'transfer his weight' rather than 'jump' because the weight of a person leaving a helicopter as small as a Jetranger has an immediate and quite dramatic effect on the way it flies. I would have to correct for that change and I wanted it to be as smooth as possible so that the helicopter didn't lurch.

I was also aware that we were all deeply shocked by what we had seen and what we were potentially about to encounter, so I took a little longer than usual to brief both of the guys on what was about to happen and in what order. Neither Roy nor Barty had spent any military time and so the civilian tendency to rush at the prime objective without full consideration of all the peripheral issues had to be gently curtailed. Once I was certain that Roy knew exactly what to do and I was confident that Barty wasn't going to try and leave the aircraft at the same time I began my approach to the tiny rock.

The helicopter performed smoothly and I was once again thankful for the strange stillness in the island air. In the latter stages of the approach I would lose sight of the target rock completely but had absolute faith in Roy's ability to perform like a professional crewman and talk me into the spot with a continuous patter of commentary. (Only the year before we had flown to Annecy in France for the European helicopter championships and had won the civilian class by virtue of our team precision work.) G-SPEY moved cautiously towards a position just above the touch-down point. To describe the next move as a descent would be an exaggeration. When moving a helicopter around in the hover with tight precision any control input is more of a thought than a movement. It's almost a Zen thing that you will the machine to a new position and the tiniest of muscle movements in the pilot's fingers make it happen. In his early flying days a pilot will execute an actual movement, the aircraft will move too quickly, he will over-respond and suddenly both pilot and flying machine are in all sorts of problems.

I felt the left skid kiss the top of the rock and could begin to use it as a pivot point about which I could control the hover. Roy waited until I gave him the positive confirmation that he could begin to extricate himself and he then very gingerly began the process. The Jetranger does not have a sliding door like the big old Wessex, it has a small and very lightweight door that hinges at the front like one on a car.

Roy's weight transfer on to the skid went smoothly and, as briefed, he carefully closed and latched the door before making the next move. As he stepped on to the rock I had to simultaneously reduce the power, once again just a thought, in order that the helicopter didn't try to jump into the air from the sudden lightness it would feel. Roy then felt his way along the side of the half-flying helicopter until he could help Barty down from the rear cabin on to a more treacherous few inches of rock. In order not to increase the gale-force wind that a helicopter generates, I remained in the same spot until Roy and Barty were well clear of the airframe and had crouched down and given me the thumbs-up. Lifting up and away from his position was then a straightforward movement.

I hovered 50 metres out to sea and watched Barty's slow and tortuous progress from the drop-off point to where Emma was sitting. Roy followed at a respectful distance. I was willing Barty on and willing him to give me a thumbs-up when he reached her position, but it was not to be. As we would later confirm, poor Emma had gone just one step too close to the cliff edge, which had crumbled away beneath her feet and sent her on the 300-foot slide to the bottom.

The next half hour exists only in snapshots in my memory. I could no longer have the luxury of remaining detached from

events. I remember climbing to 1,000 feet to call out the RAF and to brief them on the circumstances. At some point Roy got back into the Jetranger, respectfully leaving Barty to spend time with Emma before the Sea King came over the horizon. I remember being irritated at how long it took them to arrive. Despite knowing that they would be moving as fast as possible I was painfully aware of how every extra second that Barty had to stay with Emma would remain with him for the rest of his life.

I got angry when the Sea King made a huge meal of getting itself into position to recover the body. All the old prejudices of Navy versus RAF came bubbling to the surface as they flew a dummy approach, then dropped a smoke pot into the water to judge the wind, then dropped another just to be sure. My anger was undoubtedly unfair and I knew they had their own procedures to follow, but it wasn't the way I would have done it and I was suffering serious levels of frustration at not having a Wessex strapped to my back.

It still astonishes me today that I can remember just about every detail of the other 115 SAR incidents I was involved in but that whole chunks of Emma's day have disappeared. It used to be dull to always finish a flight by meticulously writing down the details in the pilot's flying logbook but I've latterly learned to be grateful for those details. It's therefore only my log that confirms that by 12.30 I was on my way back to our fuel supply at Hartland Point and from there on to Berkshire. Roy shared the front cockpit and Barty sat quietly in the back. Some of the aviation details served to distract us (all three of us being pilots) from the hard task ahead of Barty.

I do very clearly remember landing on the lawn at Shottesbrooke House to collect Sir John (Lady Smith happened already to be in Devon on business and was to meet us at the hospital). Sir John's dignity in distress was extraordinary. His prime concern was for me and for Roy and his thanks for our efforts were overwhelming. I could only guess at the terrible inner grief he was suffering. We flew back to Barnstaple, a flight lasting an interminable hour and a quarter. As we landed on the lawn of the hospital, Barty and his father thanked us once again and I remember a very new feeling of being connected with the events that were *about* to happen in the hospital, as opposed to the usual feeling of having completed my part of the task and having the luxury of leaving it all behind. The following day G-SPEY and I were back at the hospital in order to take the family across to Lundy Island where they would spend some quiet time together at the spot of Emma's accident.

Emma was buried in the family chapel at Shottesbrooke House in a ceremony attended by literally hundreds of people, as is so often the case with those who die young. It wasn't the first time I'd been to a funeral but it was certainly the first time I'd been to the funeral of somebody with whose demise I had been intimately associated in the helicopter role. It gave me pause to think.

Some weeks later the Smith family presented us with the most beautiful gift, a solid silver hand-crafted model of G-SPEY. It took pride of place on the cabinet in Roy's office, became a symbol of times shared and a constant reminder of Emma and the day she took just one step too far.

FILM PILOT

IT'S SAID THAT AN EX-MILITARY MAN has spent the first part of his life feeling like a civilian in uniform and goes on to feel for the rest of his life that he's a military man in civvies. So it has proved to be the case for me. Not so long ago it was a requirement that all young men should serve three years in the military, as is still the case in some countries today. There are arguments both for and against that system and there is no doubt that anyone's opinion on the subject will be heavily coloured by their own experience. I count myself very lucky to have never gone to war. My time in uniform was spent learning the ropes, learning to fly and then putting those skills to work in a role that felt worthwhile in the saving, rather than the taking, of lives. I'm sure that if I'd been to the Falklands, Iraq, Afghanistan, or any one of the other conflicts around the world in the last thirty years I'd feel very differently about it all, but the fact remains that I had a wonderful eight years serving before the mast and wouldn't change any of it. It gave me a trade that I still practise today, instilled confidence in a spotty teenager, taught me strength in the face of adversity and gave me the ability to work through a problem, however frightening, with logic and methodology until a successful conclusion can been reached. In short, it was the making of the man.

Once out, there's a serious danger of retreating into past glories and boring everybody to death with long stories to which they cannot relate. Thankfully, as I drew my last month's salary from the public purse, I was about to embark on a new career that would lead me into circumstances that were just as demanding and full of equally entertaining adventures, but it did feel like agoraphobia at the time. For eight years my every waking hour had been defined and dictated by others. Suddenly I had to begin thinking and planning for myself, and it felt very alien at first. The big hurdle came in 1982 when most of the people I had spent so many happy years with got into their helicopters, flew them on to ships and sailed south to the conflict in the Falklands. It felt strange not to be going with them and somehow dirty to be conducting a commercial life while they headed south, some of them never to return.

I soon settled into the new job and every day brought new experiences as I learned how to use a helicopter in the civilian commercial role. I'd occasionally get pangs of nostalgia when the media reported the successful completion of a particularly challenging rescue flight out of the old base at Culdrose or when one of the old team dropped by our new hangar to chew the fat and gossip about old mates. It sometimes felt like they had come to look at a strange new animal in the zoo but since they all concluded the visit with a request for a job when they came out of the Navy I guess the syndrome of the other man's grass always being greener was coming into play.

In early 1982 Cornwall was hit by a freakish ice storm that just about wrecked the infrastructure of the electricity lines throughout the county. This resulted in a two-month contract to fly along the lines and report the faults. We employed Ted Webber to be the observer; a man who had only recently retired from doing the job full-time and therefore knew the role back to front. For 300 flying hours I flew no more than 100 feet above the ground and concentrated on which direction Ted was looking, rather than which way the aircraft was pointing. Without knowing it at the time these were the skills required of a film pilot whose task it is to concentrate on which way the camera is pointing and simply use the helicopter as a means of moving the camera position. As an increasing number of film companies began to use us for work in the glorious landscapes of South-West England I gradually found myself forging a career path that I don't think I'd previously known existed, but it was one into which I jumped with relish. I was becoming a film pilot.

In many ways film flying contained elements of life that I was already comfortable with. I'd pack a bag, sometimes knowing that I'd be away for a long stretch, sometimes just for a few days. Once on the job there would be a large number of people working together as a team to achieve a common objective, all of whom were there because they were at the top of their profession and could be relied upon to get the job done without causing stress to the rest of the team. The organisation was generally impeccable and the catering was outstanding.

Initially the film work was principally confined to Cornwall and the south-west, an environment I knew so well from the air that I could easily come up with suggested locations to fulfil any given set of requirements. Tasks varied from filming a local documentary about a shepherd who had walked his sheep the length of the country to major car commercials for the likes of Ford and BMW. Commercials for the television were my first introduction into the excesses of advertising. The producers of a commercial for insurance came to our patch to shoot a script about a guy who had left the handbrake off and allowed his car to roll over the edge of a clifftop – which brought back a few memories. In order to leave room for error they'd brought along five identical yellow cars. While waiting for my turn to get airborne and shoot the long drop I took a glance inside one of the cars expecting to see an empty shell. But no, it was a complete car straight out of the factory, ready for the forecourt, with engine, leather seats and stereo system. Three of the five cars plummeted to an early end before the director declared himself happy with the visual effect.

As time went by the various production teams who had come to Cornwall and enjoyed using us would ask us to go further and further afield. Even if the cost of having us fly hundreds of miles to the location was high, it was as nothing compared to the cost of hiring a local helicopter pilot who was used to flying from A to B and would thus cost the production tens of thousands of pounds in lost time while they struggled with the film task. The great fear of all producers was being on location and being unable to complete the film script as envisaged by the director. In this regard the helicopter shot was always a big risk for them so they paid for us to fly the long distances as a form of insurance for themselves, knowing that we'd get the job done. I'd frequently find myself flying the length of the country to shoot just one small sequence that would end up as no more than a couple of seconds in the final cut.

My first feature film experience took me straight to the top with a week of work on the James Bond movie *A View to a Kill*. If you've seen the film then you'll remember the sequence of the Zorin Industries airship flying over the Golden Gate Bridge in San Francisco. I'm sorry to tell you that although I shot that sequence I never went to California. The airship was filmed over the waters of the English Channel just south of Chichester and superimposed in the editing process.

In 1984 I made the huge helicopter flight to Sarajevo, in what was then Yugoslavia, in order to take part in the world broadcast of the Winter Olympics. The experience would stand me in good stead twenty years later when Helifilms, the new company I formed in 1989, won the contract to supply ten helicopters for the Athens Summer Olympics. As with much of my film work one thing led to another and in the last decade we have supplied all of the broadcast helicopters for the Asian Games in Qatar, the Commonwealth Games in Melbourne and the Soccer World Cup in South Africa.

At the end of the 1980s I flew my last passenger trip and concentrated entirely on film work. I'd been subcontracted by another helicopter company to fly an executive from London to Paris for the day, in order that he could have lunch with his daughter. He had requested the fast, sleek, twin-engined (and expensive) Agusta 109 for the trip. When we met at Battersea Heliport I warned him that the weather over Northern France was not looking good and it would be fifty-fifty whether we could complete the journey. Never the less he wanted to give it a try and so we set off into the gloom and the drizzle. The weather over the Channel turned out to be better than I expected but soon after Calais the forecasters were proved correct as the cloud base came down and the rain increased. The weather reports out of Paris precluded the choice of climbing higher and making an approach into the capital on instruments so I was forced to grope my way along at lower and lower levels. When I'd got to the stage of following a line of electricity pylons I suddenly woke up and asked myself what on earth I thought I was doing. I wasn't a rescue pilot any more and there were no lives at stake other than mine and my passenger's, so I took the right decision, albeit about thirty minutes later than I should have, and diverted to a French airfield for fuel and a reassessment of the weather.

The resultant tirade of abuse from the passenger left me dumbfounded. Had it not been for my loyalty to the other company that had given me the job I would have left him right there and then to find his own way to wherever he wanted to go. As it was I confined myself to telling him that our survival somewhat outweighed the need for him to increase his fat arse with a lunch in Paris and that I was off back to London if he wanted to join me. From that day forwards I have enjoyed a life of film flying, largely in beautiful weather.

One of the contracts that provided the backbone to the film work during my ten years at Castle Air was for a 'cult' light entertainment show for television called *Treasure Hunt*, presented for many years by the lovely Anneka Rice, and then the former tennis player Annabel Croft, who stepped in to present the last series when Annie fell pregnant with her first child. Each year we would supply two helicopters for up to two months, hurtling around the country chasing clues for the contestants back in the studio. It was an early lesson in the difficulties associated with getting a broadcast signal back to the ground from a helicopter although in those days we only sent the voice signal and cut it together with the 'live' pictures later. On the final broadcast of the series I met Sara Hine, an incredibly switched-on researcher who made my organisational task a dream. By 1989 we had formed our company, Helifilms, and in 1994 she became my second wife. To this day we work together on all projects with Sara acting as producer and thus relieving me of commercial and organisational pressures so that I can concentrate on the aviation and the film content.

Sara claims that I stated in very early days that I wanted to direct productions, which is not an aspiration I can remember voicing but was certainly a natural progression. Apart from running the big sports gigs I mentioned, we've made many films over the years together and it's taken us to some extraordinary locations across the globe. The one that surpasses all others was filming from the top of launch pad 39B at Kennedy Space Centre just after Shuttle Atlantis had launched. On the day that we finished filming she returned to a perfect landing as I stood on the very edge of the runway. It was an emotional moment where a whole career in aviation and film seemed to come together at the same spot and I remember thinking, 'Hmm, this is fun. Not bad for a little ole' country boy born in a caravan.'

In 2011 we won the contract to supply all of the aerial filming for the twenty Formula One races around the world, another closing of the circle. In 2013 I wrote, directed and flew the helicopter on Australia's first IMAX film to be made in over 10 years, *The Earth Wins*, which Sara produced through our company Helifilms. I'd promised myself that this would be my last hurrah but then the news broke that the Commonwealth Games of 2018 would take place on the Gold Coast of Australia. Who knows if I shall be there with a helicopter strapped to my back? As with so many of the extraordinary experiences life has thrown at me, it would seem such a shame to miss it.

ACKNOWLEDGEMENTS

When my daughter Tiffany was still a small child her favourite pastime was to be read a good story. When 'Tips' reached 25 she picked up the first chapter of what would eventually become this book and exhorted me to write down the rest of the stories. I was reluctant at first; I wasn't sure how much of my time in the Search and Rescue role would be of interest to a party girl in her mid-twenties, but when your daughter flutters her eyelids can any of us resist? My son and best mate Sam, on the other hand, prides himself on rarely reading a book. If Sam reads this one, and if Tips one day uses it to tell some stories to her own children, then my job is done.

Three women have shared parts of my life. Ruth, my mum, taught me a love of words and gave me an open and enquiring mind. Charlotte, the mother of Sam and Tips, had to spend many years sharing me with helicopters. In the middle of it all she did a great job of raising two children I'm very proud of. Sara became stepmother to my kids over twenty years ago and has been the rock throughout my second career as a film pilot and director. Without her tenacity and good sense I couldn't possibly have achieved all the things that lead one good friend to remark, 'You guys just have the longest bucket list of anybody I know, and you seem to be getting through it.'

My special thanks go to:

- Janet Murphy and Jonathan Eyers for believing in the project and for fast-tracking the decision process. Also to all the team at Bloomsbury in the UK, Australia and the USA.
- My copy editor Mari Roberts for her meticulous attention to detail, her good advice and her endless sense of humour. She withheld the fact that she is the daughter of an RAF officer until the final hours of work together.
- Belinda and Wendy in the UK, to Aussie pals Adrian, Eleanor, Ross, Sarah, Martin and Jane for giving me the confidence to keep going, and for pointing out the words that meant nothing to an Australian reader, such as "tannoy"... who would have guessed?
- Paul Chaplin, an accomplished stovie, for teaching me to incorporate good common sense into aviation, to Nick Ross (who later achieved fame when he gave Kerry Packer one of his kidneys) for getting me into helicopters and to Phil Shaw for getting an impossible student through both Sea King and instrument flying training.
- Roy Flood for giving me the opportunity to slowly morph into a civvy at his expense, for teaching me the ethics of work, and for ultimately being the impetus to me in following a new path.
- Barty Smith for the many productive and fun years together in G-HELE. Also for his kindness in sharing his own memories of Emma with me.
- Mike (Mick) Wright for keeping me safe and alive for several decades by means of his consummate engineering skills.
- To Tim Fell for an all-year filming job which taught me that a film pilot needs more than a couple of basic moves in his toolbox, and for his extraordinary control of two jet engines under duress.

Most of all my thanks go to the wonderful men and women of the Fleet Air Arm with whom it was my privilege to serve for eight short years. Many of them are mentioned in the body of the book but there wasn't room for everybody. You know who you are. It was a good and special time together wasn't it?

Finally I am indebted to HRH The Duke of York, Prince Andrew, for his kindness in agreeing to write the Foreword. Notwithstanding my aversion to conflict I have great respect for the many individual helicopter pilots around the world, including His Royal Highness, who have taken their machines to war, which I thankfully never had to do.

For more information please visit my website: http://www.rescuepilot.net

little more than a euphemism for wandering around the coast and familiarising ourselves with the local names and landmarks that we would need to know instantaneously in times of stress. Our principal practice site was the Camel's Head, a tall and thin rock pillar that did indeed look like the head of a camel and rose over a hundred feet above the sea. It was close to other cliffs so it was a great practice site for all facets of cliff work. One test was to balance the starboard wheel on the head of the camel while the other two wheels were still airborne over the seaward precipice. Any form of flying when part of the aircraft is in contact with the ground is demanding. It can easily result in the aircraft rolling over if the pilot is not extremely smooth on the controls. But the starboard wheel is visible to the pilot and so he doesn't need the verbal guidance of the crewman to alight gently and safely. It was therefore a great place to build up confidence in your crew. The pilot would religiously follow the guidance of the crewman but always with the Camel and the nearby cliff in sight out of the open sliding door. In this way the pilot could judge how good a new crewman's verbal 'con' was working out without endangering the aircraft. At the same time the crewman would learn to trust his pilot and know where his flying limitations lay.

Balancing the port wheel was an entirely different matter as the pilot was blind on that side and had to put total trust in his crewman to guide him accurately. It was tough on the crewman as well because the only two ways to see the port wheel were to look out of a distorting Perspex window on the port side (not recommended) or to lie flat on the floor and peer beneath the aircraft across to the other side, with a 100-knot gale howling around the ears from the rotor downwash. At the same time the diver would monitor the aircraft proximity to the cliff. There was also the little matter of the decibels coming out of the two jet engines only a couple of feet from the crewman's head position. A normal microphone could never cope with that sort of assault and so we used throat microphones that were tightly fastened round the oesophagus and pressed against the voice box.

It was the sign of a really well worked-up crew if they could successfully and repeatedly balance the port wheel on the Camel's Head. When my old friend and colleague Albie Fox took his crew to that location and succeeded in balancing the *tail* wheel on the tall rock, he upped the ante for us all. The slightest error on anybody's part could have had disastrous consequences, but of course if Albie could do it then those of us with total crew confidence had to have a go. I vividly remember the elation on achieving it, but the downward bounce it induced in the cockpit was both weird and alarming.

After a successful SAREX we would wind down with a low pass over the nudist beach. It was rare to see anybody under about sixty lounging in the sunshine but there was always the slightest promise one might encounter a 25-year-old beauty in urgent need of a skilled helicopter crew to get her out of difficulties. Just doing our job...

On one occasion we were diverted from our return journey to the rescue of yet another fisherman stranded on the rocks at the base of a cliff. Halfway up the side of that cliff lay the unique Minack Theatre, a wonderful carved-out amphitheatre in the style of the old Greek playhouses. On a warm summer's afternoon or evening it was a real treat to take a picnic hamper and a bottle of fine wine to whatever the day's performance might be. It didn't really matter whether the play was a modern farce or a Shakespearian classic since the real experience was being in that location with the English Channel stretching as far as the eye could see, often as the sun went down. The rescue was unremarkable but the effect of being watched by an audience of several hundred in their seats, plus the costumed cast of *A Midsummer Night's Dream* leaning over the stone balustrade, was nothing short of surreal.

The most extraordinary thing about summer rescues was that we almost never received any thanks. In the winter you could rely upon receiving a kind letter from the recipient of our work, or from their parents, or from their company. But in the summer it seemed that the tourists regarded it as some sort of right that they should be able to get themselves into life-threatening situations and then ask others to put their own lives at risk in order to save them.

Two incidents particularly stand out in this regard. On the negative side, we once rescued a woman who was stuck on a sandbank. The tide was rising and the small but solid mound she was confined to was rapidly becoming quicksand. The routine operation ended successfully when Scouse descended from the heavens, slipped the double-lift strop under her arms and we conveyed her to the clifftop and into the loving arms of her husband. The next day the captain at Culdrose received a letter from the husband complaining that 'during the rescue of my wife yesterday the helicopter crew omitted to recover the new and very expensive shoes she had only purchased the day before'. Quite what she thought she was doing on a sandbank in her expensive new shoes one can only wonder. Presumably it was a ploy in preparation for an insurance claim but, either way, the captain thought it was hilarious and presented us with the framed letter for the squadron wall.

On the other side of that equation the crew who were unfortunate enough to spend Christmas Day as the duty SAR crew could always look forward to receiving a bottle of scotch. This was a unique and fabled event. Some years earlier a crew had tried to save an old man's wife but had failed. I have no idea of the details because it had happened many years before I became a SAR pilot. Despite the tragic loss he would present himself at the airfield gates every Christmas morning with a wrapped bottle of scotch in hand and a message that read: 'With thanks for trying.'

Medically we pilots were fit, as confirmed twice a year by a thorough check-up, but physically the divers were way ahead of us in strength and athleticism. The most exercise any of us took as pilots was the run from crewroom to aircraft. For the rest of the time we were either sitting in the crewroom, sitting in the helicopter, eating a fry-up or smoking. The latter must seem strange to today's sensibilities but I'm talking about a time when it was not only accepted but perfectly natural to smoke in your place of work or during a dinner party. We wouldn't, of course, smoke while flying: far too much to do and plenty of fuel and oil slopping around. However, one of the other roles of the Wessex at that time was in the employ of the royal flight out of RAF Benson in Oxfordshire. The airframes used for the daily transport of their royal highnesses and the upper echelons of government had a modified routing of the fuel pipes in order to avoid the cabin and thus allow Princess Margaret to smoke in the air.

On the first day of joining the Royal Navy part of the routine, during the collection of uniform, was to sign a form declaring whether you were a smoker or not. I guess it's no longer practice, but it certainly was then. If you were a declared smoker then the Navy kindly issued a carton of 300 duty-free cigarettes every month for the princely price of one pound and fifty pence. I had managed to avoid the habit throughout my youth and of course all the smokers nudged the non-smokers to sign in the affirmative so that they could buy up the surplus stock at the ridiculously low prices. Thus all non-smokers ended up as tobacco dealers with their lockers stuffed full of 'Pusser's Blue Liners' (Pusser for Pursar, the keeper of the stores, and Blue Liners because each fag really did have a blue line down it to prevent them from being sold to civilians). Is it any wonder then that we almost universally ended up as inveterate smokers?

The other common medical issue was back pain. The combination of a vibrating airframe, a cockpit that was once described as an ergonomic dustbin, and the need to sit very still for long hours of concentration took its toll even on a young body. By twenty-five I had twice slipped a disc and it wasn't until several decades later that